KNOWLEDGE REVIEW

Learning and teaching in social work education

Assessment

Beth R. Crisp, Mark R. Anderson, Joan Orme and Pam Green Lister

Social Care Institute for Excellence

Better knowledge for better practice

The POLICY

PP

P R E S S

swap *Itsn*

Social Policy and Social Work

Learning and Teaching Support Network

First published in Great Britain in November 2003 by the Social Care Institute for Excellence (SCIE)

Social Care Institute for Excellence
1st Floor
Goldings House
2 Hay's Lane
London SE1 2HB
UK
www.scie.org.uk

British Library Cataloguing in Publication Data

A catalogue record for this book is available from the British Library

ISBN 1 904812 00 7

Dr Beth R. Crisp, **Mark R. Anderson**, **Professor Joan Orme** and **Pam Green Lister** all work in the Department of Social Work at the University of Glasgow.

The right of Beth R. Crisp, Mark R. Anderson, Joan Orme and Pam Green Lister to be identified as authors of this work has been asserted by them in accordance with the 1988 Copyright, Designs and Patents Act.

Produced by The Policy Press
University of Bristol
Fourth Floor, Beacon House
Queen's Road
Bristol BS8 1QU
UK
www.policypress.org.uk

Printed and bound in Great Britain by Hobbs the Printers Ltd, Southampton.

Contents

Preface

This review is one of a series supporting the introduction of a new degree in social work. Teaching and learning of assessment is a core social work skill, and this review assists social work educators and students by examining the different approaches underpinning this critical aspect of social work education. The review will contribute to a *Resource Guide* for social work educators and students, to be made available in early 2004. We are grateful to the team at the University of Glasgow, led by Beth Crisp, for undertaking this review, and to Julia Phillips, Jackie Rafferty and colleagues at the Social Policy and Social Work Learning and Teaching Support Network (SWAPltsn) for their support and assistance as co-commissioners of this work.

Other reviews in this series will focus on the teaching and learning of communication skills, of law in social work, of partnership working, of interprofessional working and of human growth and behaviour.

The timescale for this review, ensuring its availability at the start of the new degree in England in September 2003, meant putting some aspects aside for later consideration. The review identifies the need for further work looking at the messages from key texts and at the tension between learning and teaching assessment on the basis of frameworks and instruments and on the basis of core, generic principles. We are pleased that the University of Glasgow team has agreed to continue working on these issues, with the aim of producing a supplement to this review in summer 2004.

Wendy Hardyman
Research Analyst

Summary

Although assessment has been recognised as a core skill in social work and should underpin social work interventions, there is no singular theory or understanding as to what the purpose of assessment is and what the process should entail. Social work involvement in the assessment process may include establishing need or eligibility for services, to seek evidence of past events or to determine likelihood of future danger; it may underpin recommendations to other agencies, or may determine the suitability of other service providers. In some settings assessment is considered to begin from the first point of contact and may be a relatively short process, whereas elsewhere it may be a process involving several client contacts over an extended period of time. These variations permeate the literature on the teaching of assessment in social work and cognate disciplines.

The learning and teaching of assessment in qualifying social work programmes tends to be embedded into the curriculum and clustered with other learning objectives rather than taught as a distinct module. As such, it can be difficult to delineate teaching about assessment from other aspects of the curriculum. A lack of explicitness as to how teaching relates to learning about assessment has the potential to lead to students considering they have learnt little about assessment. The embedding of assessment into the curriculum in qualifying programmes is in contrast to the numerous published accounts of teaching courses on specific methods of assessment to qualified workers.

Several different approaches to the teaching of assessment are proposed in the literature. Case-based teaching is frequently proposed although this can take a range of forms. These include presentations of case studies (based on real cases or fictional accounts in film and literature) by academics, agency staff or students, which may be supplemented by feedback from stakeholders including service users and service user organisations. Interviews may be conducted with, and feedback received from, actors who have been trained to play 'standardised clients'. A further case-based approach involves the observation of children and families. Didactic lecturing and various uses of video equipment and computers have also been proposed.

Learning by doing has long been one of the hallmarks of social work education, and supervised practice learning in agency settings gives students an opportunity to further develop assessment skills learnt in the classroom. While classroom–based learning includes learning component parts of the assessment process, such as active listening and questioning, which are sometimes taught in skills laboratories, there are also a number of models of university-based practice learning in assessment, which tend to involve students producing assessments under the supervision of university staff.

There is a substantial amount of published literature concerned with the teaching of particular frameworks or tools for assessment. Most of this relates to training programmes for qualified workers and much of it is agency-based. However, at the qualifying level there is some debate as to whether the teaching of frameworks and tools provides guidance or inhibits the development of transferable assessment skills.

Assessments do not happen in a vacuum and the ability to conduct assessments requires not just knowledge about the assessment process, but also the ability to draw on a broader repertoire of social work skills and social science knowledge. This includes knowledge about particular client groups and social problems, and skills pertaining to research, critical thinking and interviewing, as well as cultural sensitivity. Hence, the effectiveness of teaching about assessment may be curtailed if students have insufficient opportunities to acquire the additional skills and knowledge required in order to make appropriate assessments.

The relationship between what is taught in the classroom and assessment practice in social work agencies also needs careful consideration. While educators may argue that their role is to teach the principles of assessment, employers may want to employ social workers who are familiar with the assessment tools and frameworks currently used by their agency. For example, to what extent should assessment methods which involve a considerable amount of time in collecting and analysing information be taught if practitioners are often required to make assessments in short periods of time? Such questions demand consideration given that social workers seem to discard training on assessment which is not easily applied to their current practice. It is also crucial that social workers are able to think critically about the assessment tools they do utilise.

Several of the published innovations in teaching of assessment involved very small numbers of students and required significant resources of staff time and/or equipment. We doubt that many social work programmes in the United Kingdom, especially those with substantial numbers of students, would currently have either the staff or financial resources to implement some of these. Furthermore, the available documentation of teaching often includes little or no information about evaluation beyond expressions of satisfaction by either students and/or their teachers. Indeed it was relatively rare to find published accounts concerned with teaching of assessment that involved some degree of rigorous evaluation of impacts or outcomes, with only 11 out of the 60 papers reviewed including this information.

The existing lack of evaluation data, which goes beyond ratings of satisfaction, makes it difficult for us to recommend one or more approaches as best practice in relation to teaching of assessment. However, the following points may guide the development of good practice in this aspect of the social work curriculum:

- **Principles of assessment:** social work programmes need to ensure that graduating social workers have an understanding of the principles of assessment. While particular frameworks and assessment tools may be used in teaching as exemplars, teaching which focuses primarily on the administration of these runs the risk of producing social workers whose assessment skills are not transferable to other settings and client groups.
- **Embedded curriculum:** even if the teaching of assessment is embedded into the curriculum rather than taught as a separate component of qualifying social work programmes, programme providers should be able to articulate how learning objectives in relation to assessment skills are to be achieved.
- **Practice learning:** students need opportunities to apply theoretical learning on assessment. This can occur in both university-based practice learning and in supervised practice learning.
- **Working in partnership:** social work programme providers should work in partnership with other key stakeholders, including employers and service user organisations, to ensure students gain access to a range of perspectives around the assessment process.
- **Knowledge and skills base:** social work programmes need to ensure that graduates not only have knowledge of the assessment process but are able to draw on a broader repertoire of social work skills and social science knowledge when undertaking assessments.

1

Introduction

1.1. Background

Assessment is a core skill in social work and should underpin social work interventions. The essential nature of assessment has been recognised as being one of the key areas to be included in the curriculum for the new social work award in England which was the impetus for the Social Care Institute for Excellence (SCIE) and the Social Policy and Social Work Learning and Teaching Support Network (SWAPltsn) commissioning this review. However, it is hoped that the findings of this review will be relevant to social work educators throughout the United Kingdom and beyond. Furthermore, as assessment is also a key skill in several cognate disciplines in the fields of social care and health, some issues associated with, and approaches to, the teaching of assessment, are likely to be applicable to educators in fields other than social work.

1.2. What is assessment?

Requirements for the new social work awards recognise that social work practice occurs at different levels of social organisation including individuals, families, carers, groups and communities, and there is an expectation that newly qualified social workers will have some understanding about assessment in relation to each of these levels of social organisation. A further issue which impinges on the task of social work educators is that social workers conduct assessments for a range of different purposes, with no consensus as to the purpose of assessment.

Traditionally in social work, assessment has been about identifying deficits or difficulties rather than strengths[1], with an emphasis on matching needs with eligibility for services:

> 'Assessment' has been limited to the provision of already-available options, rather than identification of new services. Arguably, the process

of assessment should also identify options for the user not already in existence.[2]

In addition to determining need or eligibility for services, social workers also conduct assessments of the suitability of other service providers (for example, day care providers or prospective adoptive and foster carers), and assessments of clients to facilitate decision making by third parties such as courts of law. Social workers also contribute to multidisciplinary assessments of client options such as at the point of hospital discharge or for disabled school leavers.[3] Assessments can also consider the effects of oppression.[4] In the case of older people for whom there is little expectation of improvements in health or functioning, the aim of assessment can involve identifying barriers, which, if removed, would lead to improvements in quality of life.[5] While some assessments involve investigating and seeking evidence of past events, risk assessment is concerned with determining the likelihood of future incidents.[6,7]

In addition to a plethora of reasons why social workers undertake assessments, the timing and intensity of the process also varies considerably. In some settings, the assessment process is considered to begin from the first moment of contact:

> While intake is often portrayed as involving the collection of information and eliciting concerns about risks to a child, it is argued ... that intake is a complex stage of child protection intervention. It requires workers to elicit appropriate information about children and their families, assess and analyse this information and make professional judgements about it.[8]

Alternatively, assessment can be a lengthy process involving several client contacts, which begins after the initial intake procedures.[9] While assessment is sometimes viewed as preceding intervention, increasingly assessment is becoming seen as a service in its own right rather than as a prelude to service delivery.[3] There is also increasing recognition that assessment should be more than a process of professionals actively seeking information and making determinations about passive clients, and that clients should be involved in the assessment process as much as is possible.[10] Hence, in some instances formal assessment by social workers may also occur after service users have first undertaken a self-assessment of their needs.[11]

In undertaking this research review, we were conscious of the fact that when authors describe how they go about teaching assessment in social work and cognate disciplines, the meanings they ascribe to assessment may vary somewhat. However, irrespective of the reason for the assessment, or whether those who are being assessed are individuals, families, carers, groups or communities, there would be a broad consensus that assessment involves collecting and analysing information about people with the aim of understanding their situation and determining recommendations for any further professional intervention. How this process is taught and learnt is the focus of this review.

2

Methodology

To identify literature about the learning and teaching of assessment in social work and cognate disciplines, we searched on-line versions of *Social Services Abstracts*, *Caredata* and *CINAHL* from those published in 1990 to those entered on the databases at the time of search in December 2002. These databases were selected on the basis that literature we were seeking would be most likely to be identified by using these databases, based on our experiences from previous research we have conducted about aspects of social work education. Due to time restrictions and financial considerations, the searches were restricted to documents in the English language. All articles which were considered relevant were then sought. We supplemented this with a manual search, covering the same timeframe, of recent monographs and social work journals, held by the University of Glasgow and in our private libraries, which we know contain published articles on social work education in recent years.

As lengthy time lags between preparation and publication can result in information about the newest innovations not being widely available,[12] the editors of two key social work journals in the UK were contacted and asked if they could contact the authors of any in press papers which might be relevant for this review.

Many innovations in teaching are presented at social work education conferences, but many conference presentations are not subsequently published in academic or professional journals.[13] As the authors and their colleagues had copies of the abstracts from a number of social work education conferences in both the UK and beyond in recent years, these were searched in an attempt to identify relevant papers and their authors.

Another potential source of information about what social work educators were thinking or doing in relation to teaching of assessment were the listservers managed by SWAPltsn. Archives of key electronic discussion lists were searched to identify any authors or educators to contact for further information.

Information about the study was placed on the SWAPltsn website in December 2002, inviting interested persons to contact the first author. In January 2003, similar information about the project was distributed by email to all members of the JUCSWEC listserver. Further requests for more specific information were posted to the SWAPltsn and UKSOCWORK listservers in February 2003. A number of people made contact with the project, some of whom provided the authors with further contacts, new references and/or unpublished details about how they teach assessment. Staff at SWAPltsn and colleagues of the authors provided additional names of UK social work educators who it was thought may be able to contribute ideas about the teaching of assessment, and some of these people also suggested and/or provided readings to the authors.

Our final strategy, to identify relevant documents about the learning and teaching of assessment in social work and cognate disciplines, involved citation tracking. Any potentially relevant documents which had not previously been obtained were then sought.

The various search strategies yielded an initial 183 journal articles for consideration, although only 60 were subsequently found to be about the process of teaching of assessment in social work and cognate disciplines. A brief summary of each of these papers is provided in Appendix 1. The remaining papers tended to be either about assessment per se, in which implications for the teaching of assessment could be explicit or implicit, or were more general papers about social work education.

A draft report was prepared one month prior to the due date for the completion of this report and feedback sought from a small number of stakeholders. This included a focus group held with four experienced agency-based social work practitioners who are also involved in social work education in the West of Scotland. There was also a focus group with two members of a service user forum who have experience of contributing service user perspectives in education to social and health professionals.

Further details about the methodology for this research review are provided in Appendix 2.

We have organised the information gathered about learning and teaching of assessment in social work education (and cognate disciplines) under the following themes:

- assessment and the social work curriculum;
- pedagogy;
- frameworks and tools for assessment;
- additional skills and knowledge; and
- working in partnership.

Each of these will now be presented in turn.

3

Assessment and the social work curriculum

Although it has occasionally been suggested that assessment would be best taught as a separate subject within a social work course,[14] our search found only three courses which had a separate module on assessment. Two were for qualifying nursing students[15,16] and the other was a post-qualifying multidisciplinary childcare course for workers who were qualified in fields such as social work, nursing, medicine and psychology.[9] In stark contrast to the notion of teaching assessment as a separate module in a social work course is the approach adopted by the University of Newcastle (Australia) which developed its social work programme in the 1990s using a problem-based learning approach (also known as 'enquiry and action learning').[17] Theory and experience are integrated and the course is structured around current issues as far as possible. Several of the key principles on which this programme is based explicitly mention the development of assessment ability:

1. *Exploration and discovery – the acquisition of knowledge.* Through a process of exploration and discovery, students would learn the types of sources of knowledge that informed social work practice and ways in which to acquire knowledge and produce information.

2. *Critical reasoning and analysis – the process of thinking.* Students would learn to think logically and laterally to develop skills in assessment, judgement and argument and the means for arriving at an understanding of available information. They would be encouraged to think laterally and creatively in looking for new ways of understanding.

3. *Feeling and evaluation – the search for meaning.* Students would learn to assess the quality, importance and relevance of information, to judge the integrity of sources and assess the meaning of situations for the persons involved.

4. *Communication – sharing information and conveying meaning.* Students would learn to be sensitive, to read and respond accurately to what was going on in a situation. Good communication skills

will be taught as the means to receive and convey signals verbally and non-verbally, using a range of spoken, written, visual, audio, and other media....[18]

Many social work programmes are somewhere between the extremes of teaching assessment as a separate module and integrating it with all teaching. Rather, the learning and teaching of assessment tends to be clustered with other learning objectives, on the basis that "Social work educators do not have the luxury of teaching one concept at a time".[19] A not uncommon scenario is for assessment to be taught as part of units on direct practice.[14] However, other approaches have also been adopted. For example, one American social work programme has embedded the teaching of assessment in a course on oppression which is taught from feminist, poststructuralist, postmodern and social constructionalist perspectives, and which utilises a strengths perspective.[20] Aspects of assessment may also be included in the teaching of law and legislation to social work students. Preston-Shoot et al[21] discuss the necessity for social workers to understand the relevant legislation when conducting assessments and propose the following skills as essential in the assessment process:

- recognising the legal component in a practice situation;
- managing multiple accountability – to the law, to oneself, to employers, and to professional norms – through clarity about which values guide practice in what circumstances, the knowledge relevant to decision making, and awareness of role boundaries;
- collecting information and analysing it against the legal component and an understanding of role;
- managing practice dilemmas, again by reference to values, knowledge, decision-making frameworks, and boundaries;
- assessing risk;
- using evidence to advocate for a particular outcome;
- challenging discrimination;
- working in partnership with service users;
- networking and teamworking, including differentiating and negotiating professional roles, and establishing a common value system.[21]

A set of benchmarks for the conduct of community care assessment which have been proposed by Nolan and Caldock[22] are not in themselves a curriculum for the training of social workers or social care professionals in assessment, but could arguably guide curriculum development across several components of a social work degree. They suggest:

A good assessor will:

1. empower both the user and carer – inform fully, clarify their understanding of the situation and of the role of the assessor before going ahead;
2. involve, rather than just inform, the user and carer, make them feel that they are full partner in the assessment;
3. shed their 'professional' perspective – have an open mind and be prepared to learn;
4. start from where the user and carer are, establish their existing level of knowledge and what hopes and expectations they have;
5. be interested in the user and carer as people;
6. establish a suitable environment for the assessment, which ensures there is privacy, quiet and sufficient time;
7. take time – build trust and rapport, and overcome the brief visitor syndrome; this will usually take more than one visit;
8. be sensitive, imaginative and creative in responding – users and carers may not know what is possible, or available. For carers in particular, guilt and reticence may have to be overcome;
9. avoid value judgements whenever possible – if such judgements are needed, make then explicit;
10. consider social, emotional, relationship needs as well as just practical needs and difficulties. Pay particular attention to the quality of the relationship between user and carer;
11. listen to and value the user's and carer's expertise and opinions, even if these run counter to the assessor's own values;
12. present honest, realistic service options, identifying advantages and disadvantages and providing an indication of any delay or limitations in service delivery;
13. not make assessment a 'battle' in which users and carers feel they have to fight for services;
14. balance all perspectives; and
15. clarify understanding at the end of the assessment, agree objectives and the nature of the review process.[22]

In contrast to programmes which provide an initial professional qualification in social work in which the teaching of assessment seems to be embedded into various aspects of the curriculum, the published literature includes several descriptions of courses about specific methods of assessment taught to current practitioners. Many of these are short courses of just a few days (sometimes just one day) and tend to be taught in the workplace, or in partnerships between agencies and/or university academics.

4

Pedagogy

4.1. Case-based approaches

4.1.1. Case studies

Case studies enable assessment skills for particular populations to be taught while aiding development of knowledge in several content areas in a short space of time. Specific skills such as developing genograms (a map of an intergenerational family system[23]) and ecomaps (a map of the systems which interact with an individual or family[23]), including learning computer programmes to generate these, or using theories (for example, crisis theory) in making assessments can be taught using case studies.[19] Case studies involving student participation in simulations can lead to greater empathy with, and understanding of, the various stakeholders in an assessment.[24, 25] Cases can be identified by practicing social workers who are involved in formal partnership arrangements with the educational programme,[26] and staff from local social work agencies can be brought in to discuss how case studies would be responded to in their agency.[27] It has been noted that students respond very positively to learning through use of case studies.[19]

Bisman[28] has proposed a method of teaching assessment which involves what she has termed 'case theory construction'. This involves presenting students with the details of a case, ensuring that none of the players are labelled. Then comes the task of identifying propositions and hypotheses based on theories (biological, psychological and social) which inform social work practice, and by exploring how these may interact, this may lead to case planning to address underlying causes rather than the overt presenting problem. Communications with social work educators during this project revealed there is at least one social work educator in the UK who is using the process of hypothesis generation and sample vignettes proposed by Sheppard et al.[29]

4.1.2. Client review presentations

Client review presentations, which are used in teaching of assessment to nursing students at Kings College London, reflect a growing recognition that service users can provide valuable insights into all aspects of health and welfare service provision, including the training of current and prospective staff. This approach, which could be adopted by social work educators, involves students presenting anonymised case presentations of cases that they have been involved with, to a group which includes other students, academic staff members and service users or members of service user groups. The information presented by students should be that which would be required in order to undertake an appropriate assessment of the client. Following the presentation, everybody present has an opportunity to provide feedback to the presenting student from their perspective. Of this approach it has been claimed that:

> The intended outcomes are to illuminate the options available to students, following a client assessment, and to enable enhanced clinical decision making skills, towards an appropriate and user-centred formulation of care-planning strategies, which respond to client's needs.[16]

The involvement of service users at Kings involved far more than issuing an invitation to local service user groups. Service user groups were invited to nominate members who could contribute to the course planning and these individuals were paid for their involvements at the same rates as professionals. Agreements were also developed in relation to training, supervision and support of service users, standards of involvement and accountability.[16]

4.1.3. Literature

Van Voorhis[4] presents a framework for assessing the effects of oppression on individuals, families and groups and suggests that social work educators could encourage students to use the framework to explore the experiences of oppressed people recorded in literature, including biographies and autobiographies as well as short stories and fiction. While she considers the evaluation of students to involve an assessment they carry out while undertaking practice learning in an agency setting, she suggests that where this is not possible, students could assess and plan an intervention for someone in a book, film or play:

> … novelists focus in on the world of a child coping with crisis and while not intended for the education of social workers these books beautifully complement the more traditional texts. The impact of such novels and autobiographies, especially if they are turned into feature films, can be considerable, helping shape new perspectives on social problems or social work practice.[30]

When teaching group work, films can illustrate phenomena such as group formation and development, stated and unstated rules within groups, abuses of power, and group processes including decision making. Some films provide exemplars demonstrating how good leadership can work effectively with resistance whereas other films can illustrate poor leadership practices including abuse of power. Lengthy sessions may be required to show a film and discuss it, especially if the film is stopped and incidents discussed by the class as they arise.[30]

4.1.4. Observation

Observation of infants and children is a requirement of students in a number of Diploma in Social Work (DipSW) courses in Britain[31,32,33,34]. It is argued by educators who include this in their courses that observing children develops students' assessment skills:

> First year students on a social work course have found observation a fascinating and highly relevant introduction to the demands of social work practice. Above all they have benefited from learning to hold the role of the observer. They are learning to make assessments based on all the information available to them, not simply clients' conscious verbalisation of need, but also expressed in behaviour and emotion (and involving the workers' own feelings as well as those of the observed). They are developing the capacity to reflect and to think about the meaning of a situation. In this way they will be more able both to provide a more profound 'holding' or containment of their clients in the future and also to offer them an appropriate response.[32]

Training in observation has also been included in some post-qualifying training programmes undertaken by social workers:

> Sometimes assessments are focused so much on adult interpretations of what is happening that social workers simply don't see the child clearly or are able to ask themselves what it is like to be a child in this family. Observational skills allow the practitioner a whole different level by which to assess a child's situation. This includes the ability to stay with the anxieties, confusions and ambiguities in information, tolerate not knowing and adding to their understanding of the child and family, as new pieces of information are available.[35]

Although some programmes expect students to do 10 or more weekly observations of the same child, it is not sufficient merely to send students out to observe a child and expect this to result in learning about assessment. Hence programmes requiring ongoing observations of a child will often provide weekly (or at least regular) tutorial sessions at which students can discuss their observations with their tutors and fellow students.[35,36] It may also be important to teach students how to integrate their observations with other sources of data such as interviews with children, their parents and other key persons in their lives, assessment tools and parental checklists.[9]

Training of academic staff as facilitators of teaching through observation may also be crucial. This was recognised by the Tavistock Institute and CCETSW who for several years from 1989 ran a lengthy training course for social work tutors and practice teachers in observation.[37]

Although observation is one of the more written about methods of teaching assessment, this may relate more to it being a controversial method for learning and teaching than because its use is widespread. As one advocate of observation notes, there is little or no sympathy to such ideas in many teaching institutions.[37]

4.1.5. Standardised clients

One of the problems of in-class role plays is that students can become familiar with each other and act out predictable roles.[38] Hence, some American authors have proposed using what they have termed 'standardised clients' in their teaching.[26, 39, 40] Standardised clients are 'actors' trained to portray clients realistically and in the same way for each of several students. The use of standardised clients enables social work educators to ensure that students have the opportunity to interview 'clients' with particular problems, symptoms or issues they may not come across while undertaking practice learning in an agency setting, but may be expected to respond to appropriately in subsequent employment as a social worker.[26]

Cases can be developed drawing on real scenarios from clinical practice which have been made confidential. A script is developed which includes a wide range of relevant information such as the client's family background, medical and psychiatric history, current problems and symptomology, beliefs and attitudes, and any other relevant information that is available. The actors provide information, based on the script, depending on the questions asked of them. At the end of the interview, students can be provided with a copy of the information about the 'client', which provides feedback as to what they accurately identified as well as what they missed during the interview.[26] Furthermore, at the end of the interview, the 'client' can step out of role and provide structured feedback to students based on a checklist.[40]

The checklist for the case described by Miller[40] was as follows:

1. The student restated my concerns in his or her own words.
2. The student reflected my feelings.
3. The student asked open-ended questions.
4. The student asked for clarification about [daughter's] condition.
5. The student made a summarizing statement at the end of the interview.
6. The student asked if I was depressed?
7. The student asked about physical health.
8. The student identified my family stressors.
9. The student identified my organizational stressors.
10. The student identified community stressors.
11. The student identified my family supports.
12. The student identified my organizational supports.
13. The student identified my community supports.
14. The student dressed professionally.
15. The student acted professionally.
16. The student was respectful.
17. The student made me feel comfortable during the interview.
18. The student made an appropriate referral to other professional for services.[40]

Students have rated the experience of interviewing standardised clients highly.[26] More importantly, there is some evidence that suggests that the experience of interviewing standardised clients enhances the ability of social work students to conduct assessment interviews. This was tested in a quasi-experiment with three consecutive cohorts of students in one American university. The first cohort which had no access to standardised clients were compared with the two subsequent cohorts who did. While all three cohorts had similar baseline skills as rated by doctoral students and clinicians on a standardised 66-item scale, those who were exposed to the standardised clients were rated more highly at the end of the module than students who had just had access to role playing within the class group. Care was taken to ensure that raters did not know which cohort students belonged to. However, there was no difference in the abilities of students in the second cohort who were exposed to standardised clients and those in the third cohort who in addition to their own contact with standardised clients had access to videos of an experienced social worker interviewing the same standardised case that they had experienced during class.[39]

Despite some evidence of effectiveness, the costs of using standardised clients may be significant, especially with large cohorts of students. Miller[40] described a pilot study involving only seven students, and she noted that actors need to be paid for each student contact and also for attending training in both the case and the protocol for giving student feedback. Miller[40] paid her standardised clients US$12 an hour whereas Badger and MacNeil[39] paid $US25-40 an hour. Given expectations in the UK concerning rates of pay for consumers who become partners in health and social care research[41] and the need to allow up to an hour per student for interviewing and debriefing with just one standardised client, widespread use of standardised clients may require significant ongoing investments by universities and their funders.

A variation on the use of standardised clients, which overcomes budgetary concerns, has been reported in a Canadian nursing programme. A collaboration with the university's drama programme resulted in groups of drama students role playing families for the nursing students to interview. This provided both groups of students space to hone their skills by working with people with whom they were unfamiliar and from whom responses could not be readily anticipated.[38]

4.2. Didactic teaching

Although lectures and presentations remain one of the most common methods of teaching in higher education in the UK and beyond, few authors who are involved in educating social work students or practitioners about assessment advocate use of lectures. Even those who are aware that lectures can be used to teach theories and processes of conducting assessments, note that this learning is built on by students having the opportunity to apply the theory in practice.[14, 15]

Two American studies cast doubts as to the effectiveness of teaching assessment processes through primarily lecture-based approaches. The first involved 71 final year nursing students and nurses from local hospitals in an American city who had responded to an invitation to learn a specific assessment tool and were allocated either to attend a classroom presentation at the university, attend a screening of a video, or take away a self-directed manual. All participants were then asked to use the tool to assess three clients who were presented on video. Participants who attended the classroom presentation were found to make significantly less accurate assessments than were those in either of the other two groups. However, there were no differences between groups as to how participants rated the learning experience.[42]

A second study demonstrated somewhat more positive findings, but only in the short term. Lectures and discussion format with some experiential exercises were used in one-day sessions to train 350 health and welfare workers in California to enable them to assess cases of child sexual abuse. This method was used due to the need to provide training to large numbers of workers relatively quickly. While there was a significant improvement from baseline to three months post training, the effect of the training had deteriorated at six months.[43]

While teaching assessment only through didactic teaching may have limitations, structured input may be an important component in an overall strategy for learning and teaching about assessment.[14,44] As the facilitators of a one-day workshop for social workers on financial assessment noted:

> The question was how to make the material come alive in such a way that participants could sense that the issues were real and become actively engaged. We considered that this was good adult learning practice and that 'chalk and talk teaching has grave limitations'. At the

same time, we had participated in several workshops in which we felt that we had only reinforced existing knowledge. Consequently, we compromised on the format. A 'set piece' lecture at the outset with an overview of the issues was followed by experiential work for the rest of the workshop centred around a challenging and unfolding complex case.[45]

4.3. Information technology

In an era when interactive computer programs are being used in some agencies to assist in the assessment process, it has been proposed that professionals using these programs required training in the data collection process and how to screen for inconsistencies.[46] By requiring certain pieces of information in order to proceed, computerised assessment packages certainly have the power to shape social workers' understandings of the assessment process.

Information technology has been used in a variety of ways in the teaching of assessment skills to students in social work and cognate disciplines. These include a computer–aided instruction package which included sections of the video clips and multiple choice questions with branching according to answers given[47] and teaching students to use computer programs which can generate assessment tools such as genograms and ecomaps.[19] Networked computer software and hardware has been used to enable groups of students to work together on the development of an assessment tool.[48]

In one American university, small numbers of social work students were trained in using geographic information systems (GIS) which they could use in research projects to map information about agencies they were placed in. In particular, it enabled students to map perceptions versus actual data, such as in relation to client demographics or actual incidence of a range of community problems. The system used enabled integration of US census data, agency records and other survey data. In the process, students became aware of the extent of errors in some of the agency records they were trying to import into the system. Several training sessions were provided to the six student project groups, but this was insufficient for those not already highly proficient computer users, and the GIS system selected was simpler than many others that were available. Ongoing technical assistance was also provided. Notwithstanding the technical difficulties, a greater problem was getting students to understand the potential of the software. It had been envisaged that by learning the software this would occur, but in retrospect, a set of examples would have been beneficial. A further factor potentially restricting widespread application of teaching community assessment using GIS was the costs of hardware (six notebook computers and large colour printer) and software, which, although not specified, was noted as being an expensive process.[49]

4.4. Video

As part of a programme of teaching assessment skills in relation to drug-dependent clients to medical students, students were allocated to either a didactic tutorial, a tutorial in which four doctor–patient interactions were included in a 20-minute video which were then discussed by the class, and/or a computer-aided instruction package. All options took place within a 60-minute timetabled session. While there was no difference in the examination results between students who attended the different types of sessions, students expressed a preference for the video learning.[47]

In addition to being a medium for presenting pre-recorded case material, recording and playing back interviews with students can also generate powerful learning experiences. For example, social workers, psychologists and police from Hong Kong participated in a five-day training course on how to interview children and assess child sexual abuse. During this time, they learnt to use a structured interview framework and carried out role plays that were videoed. Each participant took part in three videos, playing the interviewer, child and as a monitor. Reviewing the taped interviews provided immediate feedback to participants about their interviewing style, as well as helping them identify their strengths and limitations.[50]

4.5. Practice learning ·

Learning by doing has long been one of the hallmarks of social work education in many countries including the UK, and can include both classroom-based and agency-based experiential learning opportunities.

4.5.1. Supervised practice learning

It has long been recognised that practice learning in agency settings gives students an opportunity to develop the assessment skills they have learnt in the classroom.[51] In addition to actually conducting assessments, it has been argued that supervision is crucial for those new to making assessments[52] in that supervision can provide a forum for articulating and challenging assumptions around causality of behaviour and whether or not such behaviour can be changed.[53] Supervision also provides an opportunity for students to reflect on their practice in relation to assessment, and this can be enhanced if students are doing process recordings of their client contacts.[54] However, the literature on supervision indicates a vast array of issues which are expected to be included in supervision sessions with social work students, and as there is not necessarily any consensus among practice teachers as to what they should emphasise,[55] assuming students will learn substantial amounts about assessment through supervision could be a risky strategy.

Practice learning in agency settings can also offer the potential for students to observe expert practitioners at work, and the possibilities for students to ask experts to explain the rationale for their professional actions and decisions:

> Clinical programs should provide a high-quality mentoring experience in which mentors share information about *how* they arrived at decisions as well as what the decisions are so that novices have access to a model of the clinical reasoning process 'in action'. Helpful questions to ask during assessment and intervention should be modeled by experts when training novices, both questions asked of clients and questions asked covertly – that is, the process as well the product of the reasoning modeled. Research suggests the importance of an active coaching role on the part of instructors, including offering guidance as well as requiring explanations and evaluating progress.[56]

4.6. Classroom-based practice learning

Classroom-based practice learning in assessment frequently involves students preparing written assessments. These may be of individuals or families, about whom students have been given case documentation. Alternately, they may involve students, either individually or in groups, being given guidance as to what information they should collect about a local community, and being required to collect and assemble this information in the form of a community profile or needs assessment.[57,58] Occasionally these profiling exercises are more than just academic assignments and may be the first stage of a community project.[59] For example, the Catholic University of North America teaches a course in community organising in which the social work students who participate learn about community assessment as well as policy advocacy and community intervention by the whole class participating in a social action project in the local community. This involved considerable realignment of participants from the traditional student and teacher roles:

> The outline of the course is relatively simple. At the beginning of the class, the class is given the task of defining the class project for the semester. Having reached a consensus on the problem and a way to address it, the class begins working as a task force or team. Class sessions are conducted as meetings, with the professor functioning as a facilitator as well as educator. Outside assignments are fashioned to serve the needs of the project, and due dates are determined as needed to complete the project within the semester. The shift from academic setting to task force is almost measurable. For example, instead of asking questions like 'when is our paper due?' or 'how long should the paper be?' students begin asking themselves questions like 'what written materials do we need to produce to accomplish our objectives?'.[60]

Although most examples of students learning assessment through conducting assessments involve students providing free labour, there are some American examples in which students learn about assessment through gaining employment to conduct assessments. For example, in response to a demand for more trained workers who can conduct adoption assessments, one American school of social work trained a number of final year students to conduct these assessments under supervision for a local agency, who would pay them on a fee-for-service basis.[61] Another model which has been proposed for the teaching of direct practice skills, including assessment, involved four students becoming paid research assistants on a project in New York which visited single African–American mothers in their homes and assessed their children's readiness for pre-school. Students were paired with a member of academic staff who was able to model aspects of appropriate ways of entering and respecting people's homes, as well as how to conduct interviews. As the interviews were held in areas of New York which were not only unfamiliar to students, but which they might readily regard as unsafe, working in pairs was a less threatening option than being sent out alone to conduct interviews.[62]

Another approach to classroom-based practice learning involves students being taught a method of assessment and asked to apply it to a case that they are working with. Methods of assessment which have been taught this way include single case study evaluation[63] and social network analysis.[64]

Classroom-based practice learning also includes learning component parts of the assessment process such as active listening, questioning and so on, which are sometimes taught in skills laboratories. The learning and teaching of communication skills to social work students is the subject of another review commissioned by SCIE and SWAPltsn.

5

Frameworks and tools
for assessment

There is a substantial amount of published literature concerned with the teaching of particular frameworks or tools for assessment. Much of this relates to training programmes for qualified workers and much of it is agency-based. Feedback to the authors is that many social work educators feel they are expected by employers and other stakeholders to teach particular frameworks and tools for assessment.

5.1. Frameworks

By promoting exploration of some issues or domains of people's lives and ignoring others, frameworks help to shape assessment practice, and in doing so, become part of the education process.[65] For example, Rumsey[66] is an English social work educator who was invited to run a two-day training session on risk assessment for a mixed group of professionals in South Africa. She chose to use frameworks which:

- specifically asked questions in relation to race and culture;
- recognised the impact of community on the individual and the family;
- looked at the organisational factors that could contribute to abuse;
- asked the workers to identify family strengths as well as areas of concern;
- allowed for a flexible response that brought in professional judgment;
- were not driven by lists of predictive factors derived from Eurocentric research on groups of 'abused children'.[66]

The framework for assessment advocated by Rumsey aims to encourage workers to consider a wider range of domains in the assessment process than those which they may consider the most obvious to investigate. However, many frameworks and practice guidelines have a tendency for prescription and can have the effect of narrowing the focus of the assessment process. A social work education which focuses primarily on teaching particular frameworks of assessment rather than about theory and practice of the assessment process may inhibit the development of transferable assessment skills:

> ... there is no conceptual framework which adequately embraces the range of assessment tasks and reflects the dominant themes and issues in social work in the 1990s. The increasing numbers of specific guidelines available to practitioners undertaking particular types of assessments ... and the various practice guides ... may lead to a mechanistic and fragmented approach if not anchored in a holistic model.[3]

A further difficulty with focusing teaching on assessment in qualifying social work programmes is that frameworks are not static and each incarnation may have somewhat different emphases from its predecessor.[65]

5.2. Structured protocols and tools

Social work interns at the Institute for Juvenile Research in Chicago are taught a structured outline for a telephone interview which acts as the initial assessment in the agency. This covers the following domains:

1. presenting problem;
2. family constellation;
3. stressful life events;
4. how the agency operates;
5. discussing issues concerned with seeking help from the agency;
6. making an appointment for a face-to-face meeting;
7. setting assignments for the client/carer; and
8. summarising the key issues as understood by the worker.[67]

Similarly, Franklin and Jordan[14] have outlined a detailed protocol with 46 questions (many of which have sub-questions) which is a generic assessment tool. They argue that:

The protocol is used as a teaching tool and to provide a framework for assessment. Not every question or technique may be relevant for every client, but the protocol gives students a sense of the areas that could be important for obtaining an accurate picture of the client.[14]

Others have also claimed an educative role for assessment tools. For example, the developers of the Darlington Family Assessment System claim it can be used as a 'training device' in child mental health work.[68] Elsewhere it has been claimed that standardised instruments enable research findings to be packaged in a way that can be readily used by practitioners.[69] Further advantages of standardised assessment tools are that limited time is needed to train social workers to conduct specific types of assessments[70] and that once trained, social workers can complete certain assessments in just a few minutes.[71]

Notwithstanding these advantages, if teaching of assessment involves a narrow focus on structured assessment tools, there is a risk of social workers having an insufficient understanding of the assessment process:

There are two main reasons why it may be easier to improve the gathering rather than the assessment of facts. First ... many social workers may lack the necessary depth of understanding and ability to apply theories to make sense of information they gather.

Secondly, the pluralism of the theory-base, both in terms of competing theories for the same phenomena and competing theories for different aspects of the social world, means that there is no obvious list of facts that are relevant. Checklists and the Department of Health guide do not state what theories they are basing their lists on. They attempt to take a theory-neutral stance, as if deciding what facts are relevant to a particular subject was a separate issue from deciding what theory explained them.[72]

A further concern about teaching, which involves a narrow focus on structured assessment tools, is that it promotes a "cookbook approach" to assessment.[2] Yet many concerns of and about clients do not fit neatly within formulaic structures:[73]

Used sensitively, the form could help both user and practitioner to a clearer understanding of difficulties. However, structuring the interview around an assessment schedule pre-determined the areas of investigation, perhaps sidestepping the older person's concerns or failing to capture the subtlety and complexity of the situation. Time and limited energy could be wasted by answering apparently unnecessary questions. An implicit assumption ... that the form constituted a more effective and reliable way of identifying need than the elderly person's own thinking was also evident.[74]

To encourage understanding of the client perspective, it may be important to have service users involved in both the development and training of students and professionals in the use of structured assessment tools.[75]

Instead of teaching students how to use existing assessment instruments, a rather different approach was taken in the teaching of an undergraduate community nursing programme in Indiana in which groups of students were set the task of developing an assessment tool for use with families or communities. Students were encouraged to draw on previous learning from both the classroom and from practice learning or prior work as well as their own life experience in developing assessment tools. Existing assessment instruments were also reviewed by the students. Once constructed, the students were then required to use their instrument to collect assessment data on either families or communities and present the findings in a seminar. Feedback from students was that this process had helped them gain further insights as to what was involved in undertaking assessments.[48]

Additional skills and knowledge

In order to conduct assessments, social workers use not only specific skills and knowledge in relation to conducting assessments, but also draw on a broader repertoire of social work skills and knowledge. The skills and knowledge, which are proposed in this next section, emerge from the literature which was reviewed for this project.

6.1. Skills for assessment

6.1.1. Critical thinking

The acquisition of critical thinking skills has long been proposed as an essential pre-requisite to developing appropriate client-centred assessments.[56] While it may not be possible to teach content in relation to newly emerging or yet to emerge practice situations, the development of critical thinking skills will be crucial in forming workers who have the skills to assess unfamiliar scenarios[76] and generate plausible hypotheses about these.[29] Furthermore, it has been argued that social work education needs to enable social workers to critically analyse underlying assumptions when conducting assessments.[73]

Teaching students to think critically may require a shift in paradigm from the traditional classroom where the teacher provides students with a set body of knowledge:

> To create an environment in which dualistic thinking is brought up to question, the classroom environment encouraged and supported the expectation of reflection, inquiry, and a certain amount of scepticism. This entailed providing a forum for tapping into students' inherent intellectual curiosity, while fortifying respect for others' viewpoints and flexibility of personal beliefs and attitudes. Thought-provoking comments and perplexities were elicited and examined, as well as conflicting and opposing points of view and conclusions corroborated by substantiated empirical evidence. This subsequently produced a knowledge acquired beyond the subjective realm, into a critical analysis

of the discourse based on a comprehensive investigation of the literature, case reports, and outcomes of research studies. It established a movement towards a level of multiplicity in acknowledging multiple perspectives. The relativist, comparative assessments of inferences and probabilities appeared to naturally flow, affording a sense of logic and rational thought in problem solving.[77]

The class exercises and assignments for this course were devised to encourage students to reconsider the basis for their initial assumptions, and included having to argue a viewpoint opposite to that which they had arrived with at the class.[77]

Despite the enthusiasm from some social work educators as to the impact of teaching critical thinking on the ability to conduct assessments, the findings from a recent Cochrane review concerned with the teaching of critical appraisal skills to healthcare workers are more cautious. The reviewers found some, but limited, evidence to suggest that teaching critical appraisal skills to healthcare workers has a positive impact on their work with clients, but whether this is due to better assessment skills is unclear.[78]

6.2. Research skills

If assessment is viewed as a process of gathering and evaluating information about a situation,[79, 80] then a need for research skills is indicated.[81] One approach to teaching assessment using an evidence-based medicine approach involved psychiatry residents in Canada being asked to identify a clinical problem in their current work and undertake a review of the literature to identify possible solutions. Course leaders then had to deal with the fact that course participants tended to report that their findings were often at odds with the messages they received in their workplace settings and from their supervisors.[82]

Rather than just be able to seek out existing research, another approach to teaching assessment involves providing training in research skills. Through teaching students skills in ethnographic research, it was expected that they would become more sensitive observers of other cultures and be able to form assessments which are culturally relevant.[83] Others have trained social workers in discourse analysis in an attempt to heighten understanding of assessment interviews through analysis and coding by students of their own interviews.[84]

6.3. Knowledge

The ability to conduct assessments requires not just skills but the relevant knowledge base.[85] Moreover, a pre-requisite to being able to assess for particular problems is having awareness of them.[27] As the following extract demonstrates, the expectations of knowledge on those conducting assessments can be widespread:

> The ecology of sexual abuse grows more complicated and perplexing. Poverty, alcoholism and drug-addiction, mental illness, domestic violence, adolescent pregnancies, and lack of education and employment skills all combine to complicate the caseworker's case management strategies. The journals and books may offer good research and information into the problem of child sexual abuse but the caseworker must find a way to use this information, to generalize it to diverse families with many problems and apply it to find sound strategies for protecting that child into the future. Caseworkers who handle sexual abuse cases have one of the most complicated jobs, requiring a sophisticated understanding of children, family systems, sex offenders, community resources, risk assessment, cultural dynamics, and case investigation, planning and management.[86]

Having a wider knowledge than just a particular type of presenting problem is particularly important if clients have multiple issues such as dual diagnoses of substance use and mental health issues[87] or learning difficulties and psychiatric problems.[88]

The impact of knowledge on the assessment process has been demonstrated in an American study involving social workers who had completed an 84-hour course in substance use issues but who were not working in specialist addiction agencies. One third (35%) of these social workers reported that participation in the course resulted in them being more likely to assess clients for substance use issues. Furthermore, they were more likely to assess for substance use issues than contemporaries who had not had this training.[89]

A study of needs assessments undertaken with carers of people with a learning disability suggests that it is not just the information that is collected which is important, but also having an understanding of what constitutes an appropriate context for the assessment to take place:

> A minimum requirement for a good experience is time and space for a private meeting with the carer. Practice relating to separate assessments appeared to vary between individual workers and the availability of someone to provide care or supervision for the person with learning disabilities. In no case did we find evidence of an authority providing substitute care, so that a carer could have a private meeting with the care manager. Not surprisingly, therefore, some carers did gain the impression that the process was focused on their relative, rather than themselves.[90]

Another process issue, particularly for social work students and new graduates, is knowing when to move on from assessment to intervention or referral to other services. In their longitudinal study which followed a cohort of social work students into their beginning years as qualified practitioners, Ryan et al[91] found in certain scenarios, new social workers tended to prematurely recommend referral to specialist services before ascertaining whether such a referral was appropriate or required. An alternative strategy was to:

> ... simply 'find out more' about family relationships, interactions and so on, in the hope than an answer may lie in obtaining this extra information. This, in effect, resulted in the process being stalled at the assessment stage.[91]

In addition to knowledge of personal and social problems and the assessment process, a good understanding of oneself is also required. Thus it has been proposed that in order to develop culturally sensitive assessments, social workers need training which enhances understanding of their own culture and the influence that their culture has on both their own behaviour and how they perceive situations.[92]

7

Working in partnership

Social workers and other social and health professionals are mutually dependent on each other in the care assessment process.[93] Indeed, approximately half of all assessments in an English study of older people who have or are suspected of having dementia, included professionals from more than one discipline.[94] Consequently, it is not surprising that we were able to locate a number of examples in which different professional groups, including social workers, were brought together for training on assessment[68,95]. Interdisciplinary training on assessment often brings together staff of several agencies, both frontline staff[95,96] and managers and supervisors of staff conducting assessments.[97]

While interdisciplinary and interagency training can benefit the various stakeholders, some caution in assuming this will lead to better assessments is warranted:

> … joint training is unlikely to have the desired effect until agencies and practitioners have explicit frameworks within which to operate and a clearly stated set of indicators as to what constitutes a 'good assessment'.[22]

Although the review process resulted in us identifying a few unpublished examples of interdisciplinary teaching on assessment in which social work students were participants, the published examples of teaching interdisciplinary groups all involved qualified workers.

In addition to partnership arrangements which bring together learners are those which bring together a training team from different settings. For example, Clifford et al[98] have described the processes and issues which arose when some social work academics worked with training staff in a local social services agency to develop and deliver training on assessment to the agency's social work employees. While this team approach enabled agency participants to access the latest academic thinking and research findings, there were also benefits for the university staff involved in the project, and presumably their students in qualifying social work programmes:

> Our partnership was intended to embody an attempt to minimise the gap between theory and practice. In sharing the planning and facilitating the course we became more aware of the different pressures that people were under in changing organisations on both sides, at basic grades and management levels.[98]

Partnerships involving service users or members of service user groups can also enrich the experience of learning about assessment.[16,75] Although the published literature concerning teaching assessment in partnership was again mostly about post-qualifying short courses (with the exception of Frisby[16]), there would seem to be further scope for developing this in social work qualifying programmes.

8

Discussion and recommendations

In 1990 it was observed that:

> Various models in social work give greater weight to the matter of the
> content of assessment than to the question of how an assessment is
> made; even more rarely do they address themselves to the question of
> how to teach young professionals to carry out an assessment.[99]

While no doubt much of the literature which we examined in the
preparation of this review could have readily lead us to a similar
conclusion, it is clear that, since 1990, a number of authors have tackled
the issue of how assessment skills should be taught.

The relationship between what is taught in the classroom and assessment
practice in social work agencies needs careful consideration. While
educators may argue that their role is to teach the principles of assessment,
employers may want to employ social workers who are familiar with the
assessment tools and frameworks currently used by their agency. For
example, to what extent should assessment teaching methods which
involve vast amounts of time in collecting and analysing information be
taught if practitioners are often required to make assessments in short
periods of time?[100] Such questions demand consideration given that
social workers seem to discard training on assessment which is not easily
applied to their current practice.[2] It is also crucial that social workers
are able to think critically about the assessment tools they do utilise.

Several of the published innovations in teaching of assessment involved
very small numbers of students and required significant resources of staff
time and/or equipment. We doubt that many social work programmes
in the UK, especially those with substantial numbers of students, would
currently have either the staff or financial resources to implement some
of these.

Clarke's[101] review of evaluations of in-service training programmes
within social services agencies found that the impacts of training on
practice were rarely evaluated. Likewise, we found impacts or outcomes
in relation to knowledge or assessment practice were reported for only
11 of the 60 papers reviewed. The most common form of evaluation

(24 papers) was to report feedback from participants, which in many cases may reflect how enjoyable participants found training rather than how effective the training was. One quarter (13 of 60) papers reviewed had no evaluation. Other forms of evaluation varied but tended to be about the process, sometimes from the perspective of the facilitators. While the explicitness of the following statement is unusual, it could be interpreted as being the implicit beliefs of many of the authors who have published accounts of teaching assessment in social work and cognate disciplines:

> Positive feedback from student evaluations and faculty who have evaluated the practice competencies of students in their field experience also have indicated that students emerge from ... class knowing how to perform an assessment, which includes a complex set of social work practice skills. However, data are unavailable to support the authors' belief that the ... approach to teaching assessment is an effective way to teach students to perform assessment. The authors have relied on their 'gut instincts' as teachers and the ad hoc reports of students and faculty. Despite this limitation – the lack of effective data on effectiveness – the authors believe that the approach has several strengths that warrant its experimentation and evaluation by other faculty.[14]

In recognition of the relative lack of evaluation data we would recommend that further funding be made available within the UK for the evaluation of impacts and outcomes of both innovative and existing approaches to the learning and teaching of assessment. We would also recommend that any funding for innovations in social work education include a stipulation that an evaluation occur, and provide sufficient funds for this to happen.

Notwithstanding the enthusiasm of some social work educators about their teaching of assessment, one quarter (23.2%) of graduates from Welsh social work courses in 1998 and 1999 who responded to a survey ascertaining their views as to how well their social work training had prepared them for practice, considered that they were less than adequately or poorly prepared to conduct assessments.[102] This may be due to social work educators doing less teaching of assessment than they believe themselves to do which may relate to the fact that the learning and teaching of assessment in qualifying social work programmes tends to be embedded into the curriculum and clustered with other learning objectives rather than be taught as a distinct module. As such, it can be difficult to delineate learning and teaching about assessment from other aspects of the curriculum. Feedback to the authors from some British social work educators is that they do not remember being taught about assessment during their social work training. This is consistent with claims that interviewing skills have replaced casework skills in the curriculum of some social work programmes:

> Although on paper casework content appears to be given at least equal standing amongst other methods, much of what is taught is interpersonal and micro-counselling skills, rather than a clearer notion of how a professional social worker deals with an individual's social and personal case situation.[103]

The embedding of assessment into the curriculum in qualifying programmes is in contrast to the numerous published accounts of teaching courses on specific methods of assessment to qualified workers. Our guess is that this reflects training requirements of social work agencies which are quite distinct from the demands of providers of qualifying social work programmes. Providers of qualifying social work education are expected to ensure that graduates have an understanding of assessment concepts which they can apply in a wide range of settings, whereas employers need staff trained to use the specific assessment tools and frameworks which the agency has chosen or been required to adopt. The presence of large numbers of unqualified staff in some agencies who are undertaking social work assessments is probably also influencing the training agenda around assessment in some agencies.[8]

Even if social workers have the technical skills to conduct assessments, there is no guarantee that they will properly define a situation and consequently determine a need for appropriate strategies to address it.[104] Yet, although it is not always clear how social workers learn to conduct assessments, there is some evidence that social work students do develop skills in assessment beyond that of their colleagues in non-cognate disciplines according to the findings of an Israeli study. When asked to indicate what information cues they had taken into account when assessing the risk to a child which had been presented in a vignette, Israeli social workers and social work students used significantly more cues than a sample of undergraduate business administration students.[105]

With very few exceptions, the views of service users were absent from the literature about teaching assessment. This is despite the fact that some models of assessment which are known to be taught in social work programmes place a great emphasis on working in partnership with service users rather than the dichotomy of the active social worker who assesses the passive client.[106,107] Having service users attend classes is one option[16,108] which was endorsed by the two members of service user organisations we consulted. They raised the fact that their presence at training events had sometimes forced health and welfare professionals to confront their own prejudices about 'them' and 'us'. The views of service users about assessment could also be facilitated through the development of anthologies of accounts of service users or by production of audio or video recordings in which service users recall their experience of the assessment process.[109]

While this project has sought to review the literature on the learning and teaching about assessment, there are likely to be some limitations to the findings reported herein. The first relates to whether we recognise particular pieces of literature to be about learning and teaching of assessment. While this was sometimes straightforward, a lack of clarity in the documents we reviewed resulted in subjective judgements being made. Thus it may be that others would have excluded some items from our annotated bibliography and included some we excluded.

Obtaining grey literature also proved extremely difficult, especially as there was only four months from the project being commissioned in late November 2002 and the final report due at the end of March 2003. This coincided with key dates in the development and validation of new social work awards in England, and some people approached for grey literature reported they were unable to provide it at this point in time due to these other demands. Furthermore, despite the existence of SCIE, the learning and teaching support network for the discipline of social work (SWAPltsn) and other organisations concerned with the development and regulation of social work education, we found there was no central repository which collected copies of conference papers or abstracts from social work education conferences. Nor is there any organisation that collects and can make available copies of course information about publicly funded social work programmes in the UK. Although in its role as a regulatory body the General Social Care Council (GSCC) collects some information from social work programme providers in England, it currently treats all communications with programme providers as confidential and is unable to provide any information about social work programmes to other stakeholders including researchers.

In order to facilitate information exchange which would benefit social work programme providers, individual social work educators, researchers, and other stakeholders in social work education, we would suggest the following:

- **Social work education library:** that a library/data archive which collects and distributes information about social work education, especially grey literature, be funded. This could be housed within an existing organisation which is involved in facilitating improvements in social work education within the UK (for example, SWAPltsn or SCIE).
- **General Social Care Council:** that the GSCC reconsider its current policies and practices around data collection and data dissemination. In particular, stakeholders, including researchers, would benefit from the GSCC releasing detailed information about programmes which it has approved.

Research reviews such as this one have significant limitations and we recognise that the documents we have reviewed may provide a somewhat different picture of learning and teaching of assessment than is occurring. For example, some methods of learning and teaching such as observation seem to have been written about by a number of authors because it is controversial[37] and not necessarily because the practice is widespread. In a parallel exercise to conducting this review, the authors identified several interesting strategies for facilitating social work students to learn about assessment, which received little or no coverage in the published literature.* We are also aware that many social work programmes in the UK ensure that students have some knowledge of widely used frameworks such as the Department of Health's[110] *Framework for the Assessment of Children and in Need and their Families.*

Perceptions from authors as to what is publishable,[111] and by editors as to what might interest readers,[112] can result in worthwhile innovations in learning and teaching being known only to those involved in them

---

* It is planned that some of these approaches to learning and teaching about assessment will be written up as case studies and placed on the SWAPltsn website (www.swap.ac.uk).

and perhaps a few colleagues. In the UK, we have also heard suggestions that the Research Assessment Exercises (RAE) have in the past been dismissive of research in social work education, and one can only wonder if that has influenced the decisions of some academics as to what topics they should expend energy on producing papers for publication.

Had there been further time, consideration of a number of areas of related literature would have provided greater depth and context for this review. Having focused on descriptions of the learning and teaching process itself, we are aware of a substantial related literature, namely textbooks, which for students may be an important source of learning about assessment. There are numerous textbooks that provide guidance to students on assessment, and these provide quite diverse perspectives about the assessment process (for example[113,114,115,116,117,118]). Further work is also required to explore what strategies for learning and teaching would best develop newly qualified social workers to both use and have a critical understanding of the key assessment frameworks in use within their own country or region.

Whereas this research review has surveyed the range of approaches to learning and teaching about assessment as reported in the literature of social work and cognate disciplines, future research needs to look more closely at *what* students are learning about assessment. These questions include:

- **Classroom learning and agency practice:** Is there a gulf between classroom learning about assessment and agency practices? If so, how can this be addressed?
- **Frameworks and protocols:** Which are the assessment frameworks and protocols that UK social work students are learning about? How are these incorporated into the curriculum, and what are students learning about them? How do students develop critical understandings of these frameworks and protocols?
- **Innovations:** To what extent are newly emerging forms of assessment which have been reported in the social work literature or are/have been developed in local agencies being taught to social work students, for example, actuarial- and consensus-based risk assessment systems?[119]
- **Practice learning:** What do social work students learn about assessment from supervised practice learning in agency settings? What factors facilitate learning about assessment from practice learning in

agency settings and what role is there for practice teachers in facilitating learning about assessment?

- **Stakeholder perspectives:** To what degree, if any, is there a consensus among key stakeholder groups (for example, employers, social work academics, service users) as to what students should learn about assessment prior to qualifying as a social worker?

The existing lack of evaluation data which goes beyond ratings of satisfaction makes it difficult for us to recommend one or more approaches as best practice in relation to teaching of assessment. However, the following points may guide the development of good practice in this aspect of the social work curriculum:

- **Principles of assessment:** social work programmes need to ensure that graduating social workers have an understanding of the principles of assessment. While particular frameworks and assessment tools may be used in teaching as exemplars, teaching which focuses primarily on the administration of these runs the risk of producing social workers whose assessment skills are not transferable to other settings and client groups.
- **Embedded curriculum:** even if the teaching of assessment is embedded into the curriculum rather than taught as a separate component of qualifying social work programmes, programme providers should be able to articulate how learning objectives in relation to assessment skills are to be achieved.
- **Practice learning:** students need opportunities to apply theoretical learning on assessment. This can occur in both university-based practice learning and in supervised practice learning.
- **Working in partnership:** social work programme providers should work in partnership with other key stakeholders, including employers and service user organisations, to ensure that students gain access to a range of perspectives around the assessment process.
- **Knowledge and skills base:** social work programmes need to ensure that graduates not only have knowledge of the assessment process but are able to draw on a broader repertoire of social work skills and social science knowledge when undertaking assessments.

References

1   Walker, S. (2002) 'Family support and the role of social work: renaissance or retrenchment', *European Journal of Social Work*, vol 5, pp 43-54.

2   Baldwin, S. and Woods, P.A. (1994) 'Case management and needs assessment: some issues of concern for the caring professions', *Journal of Mental Health*, vol 3, pp 311-22.

3   Lloyd, M. and Taylor, C. (1995) 'From Hollis to the Orange Book: developing a holistic model of social work assessment in the 1990s', *British Journal of Social Work*, vol 25, pp 691-710.

4   Van Voorhis, R.M. (1998) 'Culturally relevant practice: a framework for teaching the psychosocial dynamics of oppression', *Journal of Social Work Education*, vol 34, pp121-33.

5   Qureshi, H. and Nicholas, E. (2001) 'A new conception of social care outcomes and its practical use in assessment with older people', *Research Policy and Planning*, vol 19, no 2, pp 11-26.

6   Doueck, H.J., English, D.J., DePanfilis, D. and Moote, G.T. (1993) 'Decision-making in child protective services: a comparison of selected risk-assessment systems', *Child Welfare*, vol 72, pp 441-52.

7   Kemshall, H. (1998) 'Enhancing risk decision making through critical path analysis', *Social Work Education*, vol 17, pp 419-34.

8   Waugh, F. (2000) 'Initial assessment: a key stage in social work intervention', *Australian Social Work*, vol 53, no 1, pp 57-63.

9   Iwaniec, D., McAuley, R. and Dillenburger, K. (1996) 'Multi-disciplinary diploma applied social-learning theory in child care', *Child Care in Practice*, vol 3, no 1, pp 30-7.

10 SCIE (2002) *Assessing mental health needs of older people*, www.scie.org.uk

[11] Priestley, M. (1998) 'Discourse and resistance in care assessment: integrated living and community care', *British Journal of Social Work*, vol 28, pp 659-73.

[12] Haynes, R.B. (1993) 'Some problems in applying evidence in clinical practice', in K.S. Warren and F. Mosteller (eds) *Doing more good than harm: The evaluation of health care interventions*, New York: New York Academy of Sciences.

[13] Weber, E., Callaham, M.L., Wears, R.L., Barton, C. and Young, G. (1998) Unpublished research from a medical specialty meeting: 'Why investigators fail to publish', *Journal of the American Medical Association*, vol 280, pp 257-9.

[14] Franklin, C. and Jordan, C. (1992) 'Teaching students to perform assessments', *Journal of Social Work Education*, vol 28, pp 222-41.

[15] Allcock, N. (1992) 'Teaching the skills of assessment through the use of an experiential workshop', *Nurse Education Today*, vol 12, pp 287-92.

[16] Frisby, R. (2001) 'User involvement in mental health branch education: client review presentations', *Nurse Education Today*, vol 21, pp 663-9.

[17] Burgess, H. and Jackson, S. (1990) 'Enquiry and action learning: a new approach to social work education', *Social Work Education*, vol 9, no 3, pp 3-19.

[18] Gibbons, J. and Gray, M. (2002) 'An integrated and experience-based approach to social work education: the Newcastle model', *Social Work Education*, vol 21, pp 529-49.

[19] Jones, C.A and Cearley, S. (2002) 'A packaged learning process: the consolidated approach', *Social Work Education*, vol 21, pp 71-7.

[20] Dietz, C.A. (2000) 'Reshaping clinical practice for the new millennium', *Journal of Social Work Education*, vol 36, pp 503-20.

21   Preston-Shoot, M., Roberts, G. and Vernon, S. (1998) 'Developing a conceptual framework for teaching and assessing law within training for professional practice: lessons from social work', *Journal of Practice Teaching*, vol 1, pp 41-51.

22   Nolan, M. and Caldock, K. (1996) 'Assessment: identifying the barriers to good practice', *Health and Social Care in the Community*, vol 4, pp 77-85.

23   Hartman, A. and Laird, J. (1983) *Family-centered social work practice*, New York: The Free Press.

24   Mazza, N. (1998) 'The use of simulations, writing assignments, and assessment measures in family social work education', *Journal of Family Social Work*, vol 3, pp 71-83.

25   Moss, B. (2000) 'The use of large-group role-play techniques in social work education', *Social Work Education*, vol 19, pp 471-83.

26   Badger, L.W. and MacNeil, G. (1998) 'Rationale for utilizing standardized clients in the training and evaluation of social work students', *Journal of Teaching in Social Work*, vol 16, pp 203-18.

27   Costa, A.J. and Anetzberger, G.J. (1997) 'Recognition and intervention for elder abuse', *Journal of Aggression, Maltreatment and Trauma*, vol 1, pp 243-60.

28   Bisman, C.D. (2001) 'Teaching social work's bio-psycho-social assessment', *Journal of Teaching in Social Work*, vol 21, nos 3-4, pp 75-89.

29   Sheppard, M., Newstead, S., DiCaccavo, A. and Ryan, K. (2001) 'Comparative hypothesis assessment and quasi triangulation as process knowledge assessment strategies in social work practice', *British Journal of Social Work*, vol 31, pp 863-85.

30   Weinstein, J. (1994) 'A dramatic view of groupwork', *Groupwork*, vol 7, pp 248-55.

31   Baldwin, M. (1994) 'Why observe children?', *Social Work Education*, vol 13, pp 74-85.

[32]   McMahon, L. and Farnfield, S. (1994) 'Infant and child observation as preparation for social work practice', *Social Work Education*, vol 13, pp 81-98.

[33]   Briggs, S. (1999) 'Links between infant observation and reflective social work practice', *Journal of Social Work Practice*, vol 13, pp 147-56.

[34]   Tanner, K. (1999) 'Observation: a counter culture offensive. observation's contribution to the development of reflective social work practice', *International Journal of Infant Observation*, vol 2, no 2, pp 12-32.

[35]   King, R. (2002) 'Experience of undertaking infant observation as part of the Post-Qualifying Award in Child Care', *Journal of Social Work Practice*, vol 16, pp 213-21.

[36]   Tanner, K. and le Riche, P. (1995) '"You see but you do not observe": the art of observation and its application to practice teaching', *Issues in Social Work Education*, vol 15, no 2, pp 66-80.

[37]   Miles, G. (2002) 'The experience of teaching and learning in social work. The teaching of young child observation: a historical overview', *Journal of Social Work Practice*, vol 16, pp 207-11.

[38]   Will, R. and Forsythe, J. (1993) 'Family theatre: an interdisciplinary strategy for teaching family assessment', *Nurse Education Today*, vol 13, pp 232-6.

[39]   Badger, L.W. and MacNeil, G. (2002) 'Standardized clients in the classroom: a novel instructional technique for social work educators', *Research on Social Work Practice*, vol 12, pp 364-74.

[40]   Miller, M. (2002) 'Standardized clients: an innovative approach to practice learning', *Social Work Education*, vol 21, pp 663-70.

[41]   Consumers in NHS Research (2002) *A guide to paying consumers actively involved in research*, Eastleigh: Consumers in NHS Research Support Unit.

[42]   Flannery, J. and Land, K. (2001) 'Teaching acute care nurses cognitive assessment using LOCFAS: what's the best method?', *Journal of Neuroscience Nursing*, vol 33, pp 50-6.

43 Sullivan, R. and Clancy, T. (1990) 'An experimental evaluation of interdisciplinary training in intervention with sexually abused adolescents', *Health and Social Work*, vol 15, pp 207-14.

44 Nelson, G.M. (1992) 'Training adult-service social workers in the public sector: a core curriculum for effective geriatric social work practice', *Educational Gerentology*, vol 18, pp 163-76.

45 Bradley, G. and Manthorpe, J. (1993) 'The dilemmas of financial assessment: professional and ethical difficulties', *Practice*, vol 7, no 4, pp 21-30.

46 Carise, D., McLellan, A.T., Gifford, L.S and Kleber, H.D. (1999) 'Developing a national addiction treatment information system: an introduction to the Drug Evaluation Network System', *Journal of Substance Abuse Treatment*, vol 17, pp 67-77.

47 Taverner, D., Dodding, C.J. and White, J.M. (2000) 'Comparison of methods for teaching clinical skills in assessing and managing drug-seeking patients', *Medical Education*, vol 34, pp 285-91.

48 Krothe, J.S., Pappas, V.C. and Adair, L.P. (1996) 'Nursing students' use of collaborative computer technology to create family and community assessment instruments', *Computers in Nursing*, vol 14, pp 101-7.

49 Watkins, R.L. (2001) 'Using geographic information system (GIS) technology to integrate research into the field practicum', *Journal of Technology in Human Services*, vol 18, pp 135-54.

50 Cheung, K.M. (1997) 'Developing the interview protocol for video-recorded child sexual abuse investigations: a training experience with police officers, social workers, and clinical psychologists in Hong Kong', *Child Abuse and Neglect*, vol 21, pp 273-84.

51 Rogers, G. and Grinnell, R.M., (1990) 'Teaching BSW students formative program evaluation in the classroom and field', *Canadian Social Work Review / Revue Canadienne de Service Social*, vol 7, pp 99-108.

52 Pritchard, J. (2000) 'Training for conflict', *Community Care*, October, p 30.

53 Connolly, M., Hudson, S.M. and Ward, T. (1997) 'Social workers' attributions for sexual offending: implications for practice and training', *Australian Social Work*, vol 50, no 3, pp 29-34.

54 Walsh, T.C. (2002) 'Structured process recording: a comprehensive model that incorporates the strengths perspective', *Social Work Education*, vol 21, pp 23-34.

55 Crisp, B.R. and Cooper, L. (1998) 'The content of supervision scale: an instrument to screen the suitability of prospective supervisors of social work student placements', *Journal of Teaching in Social Work*, vol 17, pp 201-11.

56 Gambrill, E. (1990) *Critical thinking in clinical practice*, San Francisco: Jossey Bass.

57 Rittner, B. and Albers, E. (1999) 'Developing a group work sequence: bringing the community into group work', *Journal of Teaching in Social Work*, vol 18, nos 1-2, pp 113-31.

58 Johnson, A.K. (2000) 'The community practice pilot project: integrating methods, field, community assessment, and experiential learning', *Journal of Community Practice*, vol 8, no 4, pp 5-25.

59 Trautmann, F. and Burrows, D. (2000) 'Conditions for effective use of rapid assessment and response methods', *International Journal of Drug Policy*, vol 11, pp 59-61.

60 Raber, M. and Richter, J. (1999) 'Bringing social work action back into the social work curriculum: a model for "hands-on" learning', *Journal of Teaching in Social Work*, vol 19, nos 1-2, pp 77-91.

61 Tracy, E.M. and Pine, B.A. (2000) 'Child welfare education and training: future trends and influences', *Child Welfare*, vol 79, pp 93-113.

62 Jackson, A. and Sedehi, J. (1998) 'Homevisiting: teaching direct practice skills through a research project', *Journal of Social Work Education*, vol 34, no 2, pp 283-90.

63   Kazi, M.A.F. and Wilson, J. (1996) 'Applying single-case evaluation in social work', *British Journal of Social Work*, vol 26, pp 699-717.

64   Hill, M. (2002) 'Network assessments and diagrams: a flexible friend for social work practice and education', *Journal of Social Work*, vol 2, pp 233-54.

65   Houston, S. (2002) 'Re-thinking a systematic approach to child welfare: a critical response to the framework for the assessment of children in need and their families', *European Journal of Social Work*, vol 5, pp 301-12.

66   Rumsey, H. (2000) 'Learning risk assessment in South Africa: issues of language, power and imperialism', *Social Work Education*, vol 19, pp 207-18.

67   McKay, M.M., Bennett, E., Stone, S. and Gonzales, J. (1995) 'A comprehensive training model for inner-city social workers', *Arete*, vol 20, pp 56-64.

68   Wilkinson, I. (2000) 'The Darlington Family Assessment System: clinical guidelines for practitioners', *Journal of Family Therapy*, vol 22, pp 211-24.

69   Ward, H. (2000) 'Translating messages from research on child development into social work training and practice', *Social Work Education*, vol 19, pp 543-51.

70   Stanley, N. and Manthorpe, J. (1997) 'Risk assessment: developing training for professionals in mental health work', *Social Work and Social Sciences Review*, vol 7, pp 26-38.

71   Sheppard, M. (1993) 'Theory for approved social work: the use of the Compulsory Admissions Assessment Schedule', *British Journal of Social Work*, vol 23, pp 231-57.

72   Munro, E. (1998) 'Improving social workers' knowledge base in child protection work', *British Journal of Social Work*, vol 28, pp 89-105.

73   Buckley, H. (2000) 'Child protection: an unreflective practice', *Social Work Education*, vol 19, pp 253-63.

74   Richards, S. (2000) 'Bridging the divide: elders and the assessment process', *British Journal of Social Work*, vol 30, pp 37-49.

75   Francis, J. (2002) 'Implementing the "Looking After Children in Scotland" materials: panacea or stepping-stone?', *Social Work Education*, vol 21, pp 449-60.

76   Wissmann, J.L. (1996) 'Strategies for teaching critical thinking in pharmacology', *Nurse Educator*, vol 21, no 1, pp 42-6.

77   Burman, S. (2000) 'Critical thinking: its application to substance abuse education and practice', *Journal of Teaching in Social Work*, vol 20, nos 3-4, pp 155-72.

78   Parkes, J., Hyde, C., Deeks, J. and Milne, R. (2003) 'Teaching critical appraisal skills in health care settings' (Cochrane Review), in *The Cochrane Library*, Issue 1, Oxford: Update Software.

79   Hall, J. (1992) 'Assessment in social care: a series of interactive videodiscs', *New Technology in the Human Services*, vol 6, no 3, pp 26-7.

80   Erickson-Owens, D.A. and Kennedy, H.P. (2001) 'Fostering evidence-based care in clinical teaching', *Journal of Midwifery and Women's Health*, vol 46, pp 137-45.

81   Burrows, D., Trautmann, F., Frost, L., Bijl, M., Sarankov, Y., Sarang, A. and Chernenko, O. (2000) 'Processes and outcomes of training on rapid assessment and response methods on injecting drug use and related HIV infection in the Russian Federation', *International Journal of Drug Policy*, vol 11, pp 151-67.

82   Bilsker, D. and Goldner, E.M. (2000) 'Teaching evidence-based practice in mental health', *Research on Social Work Practice*, vol 10, pp 664-9.

83   Thornton, S. and Garrett, K.J. (1995) 'Ethnography as a bridge to multicultural practice', *Journal of Social Work Education*, vol 31, pp 67-74.

[84] Robson, K. and Savage, A. (2001) 'Assessing adult attachment: interview course with Patricia Crittenden, November 2000-April 2001', *Child Abuse Review*, vol 10, pp 440-7.

[85] Portwood, S.G., Grady, M.T. and Dutton, S.E. (2000) 'Enhancing law enforcement identification and investigation of child maltreatment', *Child Abuse and Neglect*, vol 24, pp 195-207.

[86] Cooper, S. (1997) 'The tyranny of the urgent: child welfare casework in the 90s', *Journal of Child Sexual Abuse*, vol 6, pp 85-9.

[87] Bailey, D. (2002a) 'Training together: an exploration of a shared learning approach to dual diagnosis training for specialist drugs workers and Approved Social Workers', *Social Work Education*, vol 21, pp 565-81.

[88] Bouras, N. and Szymanski, L. (1997) 'Services for people with mental retardation and psychiatric disorders: US-UK comparative overview', *The International Journal of Social Psychiatry*, vol 43, pp 64-71.

[89] Amodeo, M. (2000) 'The therapeutic attitudes and behaviour of social work clinicians with and without substance abuse training', *Substance Use and Misuse*, vol 35, pp 1507-36.

[90] Robinson, C. and Williams, V. (2002) 'Carers of people with learning disabilities, and the experience of the 1995 Carers Act', *British Journal of Social Work*, vol 32, pp 169-83.

[91] Ryan, M., Fook, J. and Hawkins, L. (1995) 'From beginner to graduate social worker: preliminary findings of an Australian longitudinal study', *British Journal of Social Work*, vol 25, pp 17-35.

[92] Plummer, D.L. (1996) 'Developing culturally responsive psychosocial rehabilitative programs for African Americans', *Psychiatric Rehabilitation Journal*, vol 19, no 4, pp 37-43.

[93] Manthorpe, J., Stanley, N., Bradley, G. and Alaszewski, A. (1996) 'Working together effectively? Assessing older people for community care services', *Health Care in Later Life*, vol 1, pp 143-55.

[94] Moriarty, J. and Webb, S. (1997) 'How do older people feel about assessment?', *Journal of Dementia Care*, September/October, pp 20-2.

[95] Hendry, E. and Lewis, P. (1990) 'Risk and child abuse', *Practice*, vol 4, pp 146-55.

[96] Bending, R.L. (1997) 'Training child welfare workers to meet the requirements of the Indian Child Welfare Act', *Journal of Multicultural Social Work*, vol 5, pp 151-64.

[97] Glennie, S. and Horwath, J. (2000) 'Inter-agency training: broadening the focus', *Child Abuse Review*, vol 9, pp 148-56.

[98] Clifford, D., Burke, B., Feery, D. and Knox, C. (2002) 'Combining key elements in training and research: developing social work assessment theory and practice in partnership', *Social Work Education*, vol 21, pp 105-16.

[99] Brill, M. and Taler, A. (1990) 'A spiral model for teaching psychosocial assessment', *Journal of Teaching in Social Work*, vol 4, no 1, pp 67-83.

[100] Clarke, N. (2002) 'Training care managers in risk assessment: outcomes of an in-service training programme', *Social Work Education*, vol 21, pp 461-76.

[101] Clarke, N. (2001) 'The impact of in-service training within social services', *British Journal of Social Work*, vol 31, pp 757-74.

[102] Pithouse, A. and Scourfield, J. (2002) 'Ready for practice? The DipSW in Wales', *Journal of Social Work*, vol 2, pp 7-27.

[103] Fook, J. (1991) 'Is casework dead? A study of the current curriculum in Australia', *Australian Social Work*, vol 44, no 1, pp: 19-28.

[104] Cooper, L. (1992) 'Managing to survive: competence and skills in social work', *Issues in Social Work Education*, vol 12, no 2, pp 3-23.

[105] Benbenishty, R., Segev, D., Surkis, T. and Elias, T. (2002) 'Information-search and decision-making by professionals and nonprofessionals in cases of alleged child-abuse and maltreatment', *Journal of Social Services Research*, vol 28, pp 1-18.

[106] Smale, G., Tuson, G., Biehal, N. and Marsh, P. (1993) *Empowerment assessment, care management and the skilled worker*, London: National Institute for Social Work.

[107] Smale, G., Tuson, G. and Statham, D. (2000) *Social work and social problems: Working towards social inclusion and social change*, Basingstoke: Palgrave Macmillan.

[108] Bailey, D. (2002b) 'Training together – part two: an exploration of the evaluation of a shared learning programme on dual diagnosis for specialist drug workers and Approved Social Workers (ASWs)', *Social Work Education*, vol 21, pp 685-99.

[109] Reynolds, J. and Read, J. (1999) 'Opening minds: user involvement in the production of learning materials on mental health and distress', *Social Work Education*, vol 18, pp 417-31.

[110] Department of Health (2000) *Framework for the Assessment of Children in Need and their Families*, London: The Stationery Office.

[111] Dickersin, K. and Min, Y.-I. (1993) 'Publication bias: the problem that won't go away', in K.S. Warren and F. Mosteller (eds) *Doing more good than harm: The evaluation of health care interventions*, New York: New York Academy of Sciences.

[112] Coursol, A. and Wagner, E.E. (1986) 'Effective of positive findings on submission and acceptance rates: a note on meta-analysis bias', *Professional Psychology*, vol 17, pp 136-7.

[113] Barber, J.G. (1991) *Beyond casework*, Basingstoke: Macmillan.

[114] Clifford, D. (1998) *Social assessment theory and practice*. Aldershot: Ashgate Publishing Limited.

[115] Coulshead, V. and Orme, J. (1998) *Social work practice: An introduction*, Basingstoke: Macmillan.

[116] Milner, J. and O'Byrne, P. (1998) *Assessment in social work*, Basingstoke: Macmillan.

[117] Compton, B.R. and Galaway, B. (1999) *Social work processes* (6th edn), London: Brooks/Cole Publishing.

[118] Fook, J. (2002) *Social work: Critical theory and practice*, London: Sage Publications.

[119] Baird, C. and Wagner, D. (2000) 'The relative validity of actuarial- and consensus-based risk assessment systems', *Children and Youth Services Review*, vol 22, pp 839-71.

Appendix 1: Papers identified which described teaching of assessment in social work and cognate disciplines

Reference

Allcock, N. (1992) 'Teaching the skills of assessment through the use of an experiential workshop', *Nurse Education Today*, vol 12, pp 287-92.

Country

England.

Target group

Student nurses.

Learning and teaching about assessment

Several different methods of teaching were used in a course on assessment. The course began with a lecture which reviewed the process of assessment and its relevance to nursing practice and after this students were encouraged to complete a health status assessment of a friend or relative. The second session involved a visit to an outpatient clinic and waiting areas where students interviewed patients/relatives about their health. A feedback session allowed students to explore communication difficulties, compare their experiences of interviewing friends and patients and to explore their feelings towards interviewing patients. The final component involved an experiential workshop in a medical laboratory where students were introduced to some common measurements and tests nurses may perform or observe that can be used to assess an individual's health status.

Evaluation

This component of the course was not evaluated separately from other teaching in that term. Students identified these sessions as one of the highlights of the term. Tutors' observations of the workshop also reported.

Reference

Amodeo, M. (2000) 'The therapeutic attitudes and behaviour of social work clinicians with and without substance abuse training', *Substance Use and Misuse*, vol 35, pp 1507-36.

Country

USA.

Target group

Qualified social workers.

Learning and teaching about assessment

Participants completed an 84-hour course in substance use issues over a nine-month period with the aim of increasing their skills to assess an intervention with clients around their substance misuse. Teaching methods included readings, lectures, case discussions and student assignments.

Evaluation

Eighty-one graduates of the course who were not working in specialist addictions settings were surveyed along with a sample of colleagues who were matched on social work experience but who had not taken this course. Supervisors of both groups were collateral informants. Study found that social workers who had undertaken training in substance misuse were more likely to assess clients for substance use issues.

Reference

Badger, L.W. and MacNeil, G. (1998) 'Rationale for utilizing standardized clients in the training and evaluation of social work students', *Journal of Teaching in Social Work*, vol 16, nos 1-2, pp 203-18.

Country

USA.

Target group

Social work students in a course about mental health.

Learning and teaching about assessment

Student presentations about mental disorder diagnostic groups were followed by an in-class assessment interview with a 'standardised client' who was an actor trained to portray a client from the diagnostic group under discussion. At the conclusion of the interview, the 'client' stepped out of role and provided feedback to the students about the assessment interview.

Evaluation

An anonymous survey of students was conducted but the sample size and response rate were not reported. All students who responded rated the experience of in-class interviews with standardised clients as educationally beneficial, and 94% rated interviews with standardised clients as a significantly more positive experience as compared to interviewing classmates in traditional role play situations. Some open-ended comments were reported including that the 30-minute interview time was considered by students to be too short. Teachers' general impressions of the teaching process were also reported.

Reference
Badger, L.W and MacNeil, G. (2002) 'Standardized clients in the classroom: a novel instructional technique for social work educators', *Research on Social Work Practice*, vol 12, pp 364-74.

Country
USA.

Target group
Social work students in a course about mental health.

Learning and teaching about assessment
Initial sessions involved input from an instructor on the most prevalent DSM-III-R mental disorders that social workers are likely to assess. In subsequent sessions student presentations about mental disorder diagnostic groups were followed by an in-class assessment interview with a 'standardised client'.

Evaluation
A quasi-experiment involved comparing three consecutive cohorts of students, with a total sample of 80 students (24 in year 1, 25 in year 2, 31 in year 3). Missing data, including that due to technical problems, resulted in findings being based on 65 cases (18 in year 1, 19 in year 2, 28 in year 3). In Year 1, the no-intervention control group, standardised clients were not included in classroom instruction. In Years 2 and 3, instruction included standardised clients in the classroom. For all students pre-test and post-test data comprised a 30-minute videotaped assessment and treatment planning interview, which were rated by qualified social workers using a 66-item competency-based behavioral checklist. Raters were blind as to which cohort the students were from and whether it was pre-test or post-test data they were rating. The study found that standardised clients contributed to the acquisition of students' assessment skills over and above that provided by traditional role play.

Reference

Bailey, D. (2002) 'Training together: an exploration of a shared learning approach to dual diagnosis training for specialist drugs workers and Approved Social Workers (ASWs)', *Social Work Education*, vol 21, pp 565-81.

Country

England.

Target group

Mental health social workers and drugs workers.

Learning and teaching about assessment

Training on assessment of dual diagnosis of mental health and substance misuse was jointly taught to mental health social workers and drugs workers as part of a four-day Illicit Drugs and Mental Health Training Course taught by the Department of Social Policy and Social Work at Birmingham University. Teaching involved a mixture of interactive sessions and didactic input with opportunities for professionals from different agencies and professional backgrounds to work together in exploring their responses to a variety of case scenarios.

Evaluation

This is the first of two linked papers. The evaluation is presented in the second paper.

Reference

Bailey, D. (2002) 'Training together – part two: an exploration of the evaluation of a shared learning programme on dual diagnosis for specialist drug workers and Approved Social Workers (ASWs)', *Social Work Education*, vol 21, pp 685-99.

Country

England.

Target group

Mental health social workers and drugs workers.

Learning and teaching about assessment

A training needs analysis had identified a need for a balance between uni-disciplinary and shared learning inputs. Shared teaching included input from service users. Each day of 4-5 day courses included a mix of didactic teaching, case study exercises, problem-solving tasks and experiential exercised.

Evaluation

Four courses were delivered over a two-year period with a total of 92 participants. A detailed evaluation was conducted which examined curriculum content, training methods and design, learners' satisfaction, and practice outcomes but with a key emphasis on the process of delivering training in an interprofessional context.

Reference
Baldwin, M. (1994) 'Why observe children?', *Social Work Education*, vol 13, pp 74-85.
Country
England.
Target group
Social work students.
Learning and teaching about assessment
This paper makes a case for the inclusion of child observation as a core component of social work training in the DipSW, arguing that observation skills are essential for both assessing individuals and their settings, as well as promoting anti-oppressive practice.
Evaluation
Positive student feedback.

Reference
Bending, R.L. (1997) 'Training child welfare workers to meet the requirements of the Indian Child Welfare Act', *Journal of Multicultural Social Work*, vol 5, pp 151-64.
Country
USA.
Target group
Child welfare personnel who deliver child welfare or child protection services to Native American children and their families.
Learning and teaching about assessment
Four modules were developed to provide training to support implementation of the Indian Child Welfare Act (ICWA) in the state of Washington. Module 1 aimed to develop collaborative relationships between child welfare workers by pairing tribal and state workers in the same service area. Module 2 was about tribal and state workers enhancing their knowledge and understanding of one another's work environment, policies and procedures. Module 3 focused on culturally appropriate methods of assessment, intervention and

prevention of child abuse in American Indian communities. Module 4 provided further information about the intent, definitions, and procedures of the ICWA.

Evaluation

Pre-test and post-test data was sought from the 34 participants, with both sets of data available from 23. Post-test data found some increases in knowledge about the ICWA and changes in attitudes and practices in relation to complying with this legislation. Semi-structured follow-up interviews were later conducted with 16 participants to gain further insights from participants about the course and how they have used the information gained in the course in their practice.

Reference

Bilsker, D. and Goldner, E.M. (2000) 'Teaching evidence-based practice in mental health', *Research on Social Work Practice*, vol 10, pp 664-9.
Reprinted from *Evidence-based Mental Health*, vol 2, pp 68-9.

Country

Canada.

Target group

Psychiatry residents in a postgraduate training programme.

Learning and teaching about assessment

Training in evidence-based practice included concepts such as classification of studies and publications and assessment levels of evidence; the hypothesis testing/falsificationist model of research; randomisation; control groups; blinding; the use of statistical tests; statistical power and how it can be determined; study design; and justification of conclusions. Participants were then asked to identify a clinical problem in their current work and undertake a review of the literature to identify possible solutions.

Evaluation

Feedback from participants was reported.

Reference

Bisman, C.D. (2001) 'Teaching social work's bio-psycho-social assessment', *Journal of Teaching in Social Work*, vol 21, nos 3-4, pp 75-89.

Country

USA.

Target group

Social work students.

Learning and teaching about assessment

A method of teaching assessment which the author terms 'case theory construction' is proposed. This involves presenting students with the details of a case, taking care not to label any of the players. Then comes the task of identifying propositions and hypotheses based on theories (biological, psychological and social) which inform social work practice, and by exploring how these may interact, this may lead to case planning to address underlying causes rather than the overt presenting problem.

Evaluation

No evaluation provided.

Reference

Bradley, G. and Manthorpe, J. (1993) 'The dilemmas of financial assessment: professional and ethical difficulties', *Practice*, vol 7, no 4, pp 21-30.

Country

England.

Target group

Thirty-two care management staff from a local authority in the north of England participated in this training course.

Learning and teaching about assessment

A one-day workshop on financial assessment began with a presentation about the legal context, including indicators of financial abuse, system responses to individuals unable to control their own finances, and disability benefits. The remainder of the day involved small groups working through a challenging and unfolding case, with new information being provided to the groups throughout the day.

Evaluation

Feedback sheets were completed by 25 participants. These included a series of statements which participants were asked to respond on a four-point scale as to the extent of their agreement or disagreement with each statement. There was also space for participants to make their own comments. Participants all agreed and the majority strongly so, that the aims of the day were clear, that the event was well organised, that the workshop was useful to practice and that it increased knowledge of financial assessment.

Reference

Brill, M. and Taler, A. (1990) 'A spiral model for teaching psychosocial assessment', *Journal of Teaching in Social Work*, vol 4, no 1, pp 67-83.

Country

Israel.

Target group

Social work students.

Learning and teaching about assessment

A method of teaching about psychosocial assessment to social work students is proposed which aims to encourage scientific thinking about assessment. The model proposes students collect data in five domains: (1) the family picture; (2) reasons for seeking help, (3) coping patterns at the individual and family levels; (4) coping patterns at the societal level; and (5) coping patterns in formal settings. At each stage students are encouraged to collect relevant data, consider information in relation to relevant theory, and develop hypotheses and test these. The integration of data from the various domains results in an assessment from which planning for further intervention can be based.

Evaluation

The authors report having used this model in their own teaching and that feedback from students indicated that it helped them to appreciate the significance that their theoretical studies have for casework.

Reference

Burman, S. (2000) 'Critical thinking: its application to substance abuse education and practice', *Journal of Teaching in Social Work*, vol 20, nos 3-4, pp 155-72.

Country

USA.

Target group

Social work students in a course on substance use.

Learning and teaching about assessment

The development of critical thinking skills is proposed as an essential pre-requisite to developing appropriate client-centred assessments. Class exercises and assignments for this course were devised to encourage students to reconsider the basis for their initial assumptions, and included having to argue a viewpoint opposite to that which they had arrived with at the class.

Evaluation

Pre-test and post-test ratings on attitude scales were completed by 28 students and these revealed some changes in student beliefs and attitudes. Some additional comments from students as to how the course has changed their thinking about substance use are reported.

Reference

Burrows, D., Trautmann, F., Frost, L., Bijl, M., Sarankov, Y., Sarang, A. and Chernenko, O. (2000) 'Processes and outcomes of training on rapid assessment and response methods on injecting drug use and related HIV infection in the Russian Federation', *International Journal of Drug Policy*, vol 11, pp 151-67.

Country

Russia.

Target group

Health professionals. Participants from each city are accepted in groups of three, with one participant from a government AIDS organisation, one from a government drug and alcohol setting and one from a non-government setting.

Learning and teaching about assessment

Eighty-nine Russian health professionals were trained in the use of the WHO's Rapid Assessment and Response Guide on Injecting Drug Use. The training programme includes participants carrying out a rapid situation assessment (RSA) as a step towards designing and implementing an effective programme to prevent HIV transmission among injecting drug users. Each course took place over 4 months, beginning with an initial training course (11-12 days) followed by 12 weeks work in which participants carry out assessments in their own cities, followed by a further 5-6 days training on using assessment findings and programme planning. Where possible, trainers would do city visits during the fieldwork period. The last day of the initial training course involved participants hearing the results of students who were on the Return Training Course. The rapid assessment process involves obtaining varying types of data from sources such as government agencies, hospitals and health centres, client groups, prisoners, general population surveys, school students, as well as quantitative data which might include focus groups, observations, semi-structured interviews and analysis of news media.

Evaluation

Authors' observations from the first four training cycles (January 1998 to January 1999) which involved 89 health professionals from 32 Russian cities.

An overview of the problems faced by participants undertaking rapid assessments is provided as is some information about the 14 harm reduction programmes which resulted from these assessments.

Reference

Cheung, K.M. (1997) 'Developing the interview protocol for video-recorded child sexual abuse investigations: a training experience with police officers, social workers, and clinical psychologists in Hong Kong', *Child Abuse and Neglect*, vol 21, pp 273-84.

Country

Hong Kong.

Target group

Social workers (31), police officers (36) and clinical psychologists (7) involved in child sexual abuse investigations.

Learning and teaching about assessment

During a five-day training course on how to interview children and assess child sexual abuse participants learnt how to use a structured interview framework and conducted role plays which were video-taped. The interview protocol involved four stages: rapport building, free narrative or account, questioning, and closure. Each participant took part in three videos, playing the interviewer, child and as a monitor, and playing back the taped interviews provided immediate feedback to participants about their interviewing style, as well as helping them identify their strengths and limitations.

Evaluation

Content analysis of 74 role-played interviews of video-recorded investigation revealed 119 questions and statements that were rated by the professionals and their instructor as helpful techniques in interviewing children suspected of having been sexually abused. Differences were revealed between police techniques and those used by social workers and psychologists.

Reference

Clifford, D., Burke, B., Feery, D. and Knox, C. (2002) 'Combining key elements in training and research: developing social work assessment theory and practice in partnership', *Social Work Education*, vol 21, pp 105-16.

Country

England.

Target group

Child and family social workers employed by a local authority.

Learning and teaching about assessment

Developed as a training and research course in 1997 by a group that included social work academics and training staff from a local authority social work department. A pilot course run in 1998 and four further courses subsequently conducted, with some modifications in methods of presentation for the four-day course. The first two days were devoted to understanding basic methodological issues and anti-oppressive values in social work assessment. The following two days, which occurred a couple of week later, were centred on the narrower issues of using specific forms of assessment in childcare in the critical light of a grasp of the methodology, focusing particularly on needs assessments and risks assessments and drawing on their own cases.

Evaluation

Social worker, social services and university perspectives were obtained on the process.

Reference

Costa, A.J. and Anetzberger, G. (1997) 'Recognition and intervention for elder abuse', *Journal of Aggression, Maltreatment and Trauma*, vol 1, pp 243-60.

Country

USA.

Target group

Students of medicine, nursing, psychology or social work.

Learning and teaching about assessment

A strategy for teaching students about elder abuse is proposed. An introductory lecture about elder abuse should be followed by case discussions (details of three cases are provided) to which local professionals (for example, doctors and social workers) should be invited to give their professional perspectives.

Evaluation

No evaluation provided.

Reference

Dietz, C.A. (2000) 'Reshaping clinical practice for the new millennium', *Journal of Social Work Education*, vol 36, pp 503-20.

Country

USA.

Target group

Social work students.

Learning and teaching about assessment

Teaching of assessment is embedded in a course on oppression which is taught from feminist, poststructuralist, postmodern and social constructionalist perspectives, and which utilises a strengths perspective.

Evaluation

Reported that student feedback has been consistently positive. A small sample (20) responded to additional informal survey, of whom 90% found the material on oppression and abuse helpful. Only two students found the focus on oppression and abuse to be excessive or inappropriate.

Reference

Erickson-Owens, D.A. and Kennedy, H.P. (2001) 'Fostering evidence-based care in clinical teaching', *Journal of Midwifery and Women's Health*, vol 46, pp 137-45.

Country

USA.

Target group

Midwifery students.

Learning and teaching about assessment

The authors aim to foster evidence-based care through clinical teaching which encourages students to (1) ask the question; (2) locate the evidence; (3) appraise the evidence; and (4) act on the evidence.

Evaluation

None.

Reference
Flannery, J. and Land, K. (2001) 'Teaching acute care nurses cognitive assessment using LOCFAS: what's the best method?', *Journal of Neuroscience Nursing*, vol 33, pp 50-6.

Country
USA.

Target group
Final year nursing students and qualified nurses.

Learning and teaching about assessment
Seventy-one final year nursing students and nurses from local hospitals in an American city who had responded to an invitation to learn the Levels of Cognitive Functioning Assessment Scale (LOCFAS) were allocated either to attend a classroom presentation at the university, attend a screening of a video, or take away a self-directed manual depending on the time slot participants signed up to attend.

Evaluation
All participants were asked to use the tool to assess three clients who were presented on video. All three methods used produced acceptable results, but the more control the learner had, the better the outcomes. However, there were no differences between groups as to how participants rated the learning experience.

Reference
Franklin, C. and Jordan, C. (1992) 'Teaching students to perform assessments', *Journal of Social Work Education*, vol 28, pp 222-41.

Country
USA.

Target group
Social work students.

Learning and teaching about assessment
Social work students taught theories and processes of conducting assessments, including preparing an assessment report, using lectures, being provided with examples, have the opportunity to apply the theory in supervised practice learning in agency settings. In particular, students are provided with a detailed protocol that is a generic assessment tool which they can adapt according to circumstances.

Evaluation

'Gut instincts' of the teaching staff are provided, including discussion of the strengths and limitations of their approach.

Reference

Frisby, R. (2001) 'User involvement in mental health branch education: client review presentations', *Nurse Education Today*, vol 21, pp 663-9.

Country

England.

Target group

Nursing students as part of a core module of the Mental Health Branch programme entitled 'Assessment and Interventions in Mental Health Nursing'.

Learning and teaching about assessment

The aims of client review sessions are to create an effective and conducive learning environment, for students and mental health users to collaborate, and influence subsequent care delivery based on students' enhanced client-centred awareness. The client review presentation method is aimed at encouraging students to reflect on their assessment work with clients experiencing mental health problems. It involves collaborative classroom activities with students, user representatives and lecturers, in exploring the dynamics of a client assessment recently undertaken by a student in their clinical practice.

Evaluation

Students provided feedback on the strengths and weaknesses of the approach and verbatim comments by one group of students are included.

Reference

Gibbons, J. and Gray, M. (2002) 'An integrated and experience-based approach to social work education: the Newcastle model', *Social Work Education*, vol 21, pp 529-49.

Country

Australia.

Target group

Social work students.

Learning and teaching about assessment

The University of Newcastle (Australia) developed its social work programme in the 1990s using a problem-based learning approach. Theory and experience are integrated and the course is structured around current issues as far as possible. Several of the key principles on which this programme is based explicitly mention the development of assessment ability.

Evaluation

No formal evaluation of learning and teaching about assessment per se but staff and students engage in a continuous process of critical reflection during the course. Graduates and students undertaking supervised practice learning are particularly valued in their workplaces.

Reference

Glennie, S. and Horwath, J. (2000) 'Inter-agency training: broadening the focus', *Child Abuse Review*, vol 9, pp 148-56.

Country

England.

Target group

Middle managers who supervise staff involved in child protection work.

Learning and teaching about assessment

Interagency training has a key role in building and maintaining shared responsibility for planning, administering and delivery of services to children. A one-day programme of training for Area Child Protection Committees to deliver to managers/supervisors of staff involved in child protection work is described with the aim of ensuring participants are aware of the *Framework for the Assessment of Children in Need*.

Evaluation

No evaluation of the suggested one-day workshop is provided.

Reference

Hendry, E. and Lewis, P. (1990) 'Risk and child abuse', *Practice*, vol 4, pp 146-55.

Country

England.

Target group

Social workers, probation officers, health visitors and education welfare officers employed in four different agencies in Nottinghamshire.

Learning and teaching about assessment

'Working with Risk' is a three-day training course in risk assessment and child protection for probation officers, health visitors, education welfare officers and social workers from four agencies. The course involves both theory and practice and is taught through both presentations and small group work. Prior to the course all participants prepare a written outline of a case which concerns them. The first day focuses on participants' materials. Later days examine risk indicators, moving to risk frameworks.

Evaluation

None.

Reference

Hill, M. (2002) 'Network assessments and diagrams: a flexible friend for social work practice and education', *Journal of Social Work*, vol 2, pp 233-54.

Country

Scotland.

Target group

Social work students.

Learning and teaching about assessment

A process for teaching social network analysis is described which includes in-class teaching, an exercise for students to complete as part of their supervised practice learning, follow-up classes at the university and individual written feedback to students about the examples they have presented. Examples of student work are included in this paper.

Evaluation

Various forms of evaluation of teaching include student feedback on the process, class discussions and reviewing the social network analyses completed by students.

Reference

Iwaniec, D., McAuley, R. and Dillenburger, K. (1996) 'Multi-disciplinary diploma applied social-learning theory in child care', *Child Care in Practice*, vol 3, no 1, pp 30-7.

Country

Northern Ireland.

Target group

Childcare professionals enrolled in a post-qualifying programme in childcare.

Learning and teaching about assessment

The Applied Social Learning Theory Course in Child Care is a multi-disciplinary one-year programme of part-time study designed for experienced childcare professionals in field and residential social work, medicine, psychology, nursing and allied disciplines. The key aims are to equip students with knowledge and skills in child development, social learning theory, and behavioural assessment, treatment and evaluation. Module 1 covers social learning theory and child development. Module 2 is concerned with behavioural assessment and common behavioural problems and disorders and includes behavioural interviewing practice and methods, behavioural observational practice and methods, and the use of a variety of psychometric assessment tools. Module 3 is about behavioural treatment and evaluation.

Evaluation

Positive feedback from students. Some examples of student work conducted as part of the course provided.

Reference

Jackson, A. and Sedehi, J. (1998) 'Homevisiting: teaching direct practice skills through a research project', *Journal of Social Work Education*, vol 34, pp 283-90.

Country

USA.

Target group

Social work students.

Learning and teaching about assessment

Four students became research assistants on a project in New York which involved visiting single African-American mothers in their homes and assessing their children's readiness for pre-school. Students were paired with a member of academic staff who was able to model aspects of appropriate ways of entering and respecting people's homes, as well as how to conduct assessment interviews.

Evaluation

The authors recognise that a limitation of the article is that their project had no evaluative component to demonstrate the efficacy of their ideas for student learning of either research or practice techniques.

Reference

Johnson, A.K. (2000) 'The community practice pilot project: integrating methods, field, community assessment, and experiential learning', *Journal of Community Practice*, vol 8, no 4, pp 5-25.

Country

USA.

Target group

Social work students.

Learning and teaching about assessment

Description of classroom learning to prepare students for community development practice learning opportunities in organisations in which no social workers were employed. A major focus of this teaching involved preparing students to complete a community assessment for a local area, on the premise that experiential learning about community assessment was more salient than just theoretical teaching.

Evaluation

A description of the outcomes of this pilot project is provided.

Reference

Jones, C.A. and Cearley, S. (2002) 'A packaged learning process: the consolidated approach', *Social Work Education*, vol 21, pp 71-7.

Country

USA.

Target group

Social work students.

Learning and teaching about assessment

Case studies are used to facilitate learning about assessment skills for particular populations. Using an ecological model, assessment skills such as developing genograms and ecomaps (including learning computer programs to generate these) or using theories (for example, crisis theory) in making assessments can be taught using case studies.

Evaluation

Class discussions.

Reference
Kemshall, H. (1998) 'Enhancing risk decision making through critical path analysis', *Social Work Education*, vol 17, pp 419-34.

Country
England.

Target group
Probation officers.

Learning and teaching about assessment
Critical path analysis is used as a tool to teach risk assessment to probation officers in a one-day training programme which is outlined, including training exercises.

Evaluation
Participant feedback with examples cited.

Reference
King, R. (2002) 'Experience of undertaking infant observation as part of the Post-Qualifying Award in Child Care', *Journal of Social Work Practice*, vol 16, pp 213-21.

Country
England.

Target group
Qualified social workers enrolled in advanced award in childcare.

Learning and teaching about assessment
Students undertaking a post-qualifying award in childcare conduct 10 one-hour weekly observations of a 'normal' child not known to the author plus weekly seminars/discussions with other students/tutors about what they are observing.

Evaluation
This paper is the author's personal reflection of the experience of being a student in this course.

Reference
Krothe, J.S., Pappas, V.C. and Adair, L.P. (1996) 'Nursing students' use of collaborative computer technology to create family and community assessment instruments', *Computers in Nursing*, vol 14, pp 101-7.

Country
USA.

Target group

Nursing students in the final semester of a community health clinical course.

Learning and teaching about assessment

An undergraduate community nursing programme in Indiana set groups of 7-10 students the task of developing an assessment tool for use with families or communities. Students were encouraged to draw on previous learning from both the classroom and in practice or prior work as well as their own life experience in developing assessment tools. Existing assessment instruments were also reviewed by the students. Once constructed, the students were then required to use their instrument to collect assessment data on either families or communities and present the findings in a seminar.

Evaluation

Analysis of qualitative feedback from students revealed five key themes, which provided a structure for data analysis. Students reported that this process had helped them gain further insights as to what was involved in undertaking assessments.

Reference

McKay, M.M., Bennett, E., Stone, S. and Gonzales, J. (1995) 'A comprehensive training model for inner-city social workers', *Arete*, vol 20, pp 56-64.

Country

USA.

Target group

Social work students.

Learning and teaching about assessment

Social work interns at the Institute for Juvenile Research in Chicago are taught a structured outline for a telephone interview that acts as the initial assessment in the agency.

Evaluation

None.

Reference

McMahon, L. and Farnfield, S. (1994) 'Infant and child observation as preparation for social work practice', *Social Work Education*, vol 13, pp 81-98.

Country

England.

Target group

Social work students.

Learning and teaching about assessment

Infant and child observation is a required part of the DipSW at the University of Reading. This involves one-hour per week observation for 15 weeks with weekly college sessions. The authors claim that it equips students with relevant assessment skills.

Evaluation

Evaluation is descriptive and includes verbatim comments from students about what they have learnt from observing an infant or child.

Reference

Mazza, N. (1998) 'The use of simulations, writing assignments, and assessment measures in family social work education', *Journal of Family Social Work*, vol 3, pp 71-83.

Country

USA.

Target group

Social work students.

Learning and teaching about assessment

Family assessment is taught through a range of methods including simulations, written assignments that reflect professional demands as to the format and content of assessments, and use of assessment forms that require narrative input. Students are also introduced to a range of standardised assessment tools including the Family Environment Scale, the Family Therapist Rating Scale and the Feminist Family Therapist Behavior Checklist. Course example.

Evaluation

The author notes that over the previous 13 years students have responded favourably to the course.

Reference

Miles, G. (2002) 'The experience of learning and teaching in social work. The teaching of young child observation: a historical overview', *Journal of Social Work Practice*, vol 16, pp 207-11.

Country

England.

Target group

Social work tutors and practice teachers.

Learning and teaching about assessment

Describes the setting up in 1989 of the Tavistock/CCETSW course in young child observation for social work tutors and practice teachers. Participants were involved in child observation over a year, and also attended lectures and seminars.

Evaluation

Feedback from participants is reported.

Reference

Miller, M. (2002) 'Standardized clients: an innovative approach to practice learning', *Social Work Education*, vol 21, pp 663-70.

Country

USA.

Target group

Social work students.

Learning and teaching about assessment

Seven MSW students interviewed a standardised client and feedback was provided to the students by the standardised client and then two social work faculty members.

Evaluation

Students completed a satisfaction survey, although findings are limited by small convenience sample.

Reference

Moss, B. (2000) 'The use of large-group role-play techniques in social work education', *Social Work Education*, vol 19, pp 471-83.

Country

England.

Target group

Social work students.

Learning and teaching about assessment

Students (in groups of up to 25) learn about the dynamics of assessment by participating in a large group role play and using assessment tools such as genograms. This took place over six two-hour sessions.

Evaluation

Students provided written feedback about their learning from this process.

Reference

Nelson, G.M. (1992) 'Training adult-service social workers in the public sector: a core curriculum for effective geriatric social work practice', *Educational Gerentology*, vol 18, pp 163-76.

Country

USA.

Target group

Adult service social workers.

Learning and teaching about assessment

Six-day workshops about geriatric assessment and case management, broken into three two-consecutive day sessions spread over a month-and-a-half. Methods of teaching include didactic input, practical exercises, and provision of a written curriculum guide and back-up resource book.

Evaluation

Positive feedback from participants.

Reference

Preston-Shoot, M., Roberts, G. and Vernon, S. (1998) 'Developing a conceptual framework for teaching and assessing law within training for professional practice: lessons from social work', *Journal of Practice Teaching*, vol 1, pp 41-51.

Country

England.

Target group

Social work students and practice teachers.

Learning and teaching about assessment

Proposes use of case examples to demonstrate the legal skills and knowledge required to complete social work assessments.

Evaluation

None.

Reference

Raber, M. and Richter, J. (1999) 'Bringing social work action back into the social work curriculum: a model for "hands-on" learning', *Journal of Teaching in Social Work*, vol 19, nos 1-2, pp 77-91.

Country

USA.

Target group

Social work students.

Learning and teaching about assessment

The Catholic University of North America teaches a course in community organising in which the social work students who participate learn about community assessment as well as policy advocacy and community intervention by the whole class participating in a social action project in the local community.

Evaluation

Comments from both students' logs and course evaluations are presented. Students rated the course as outstanding, particularly in the areas addressing the relevance and utility of the course for their future careers.

Reference

Reynolds, J. and Read, J. (1999) 'Opening minds: user involvement in the production of learning materials on mental health and distress', *Social Work Education*, vol 18, pp 417-31.

Country

England.

Target group

Open University students in a mental health course.

Learning and teaching about assessment

This paper describes the process of involving users in the production of course materials for an Open University course on mental health. These materials aim to provide students with service user perspectives in contrast to more traditional academic materials that privilege the perspectives of mental health professionals.

Evaluation

Student and tutor feedback from first cohort was very enthusiastic.

Reference

Rittner, B. and Albers, E. (1999) 'Developing a group work sequence: bringing the community into group work', *Journal of Teaching in Social Work*, vol 18, nos 1-2, pp 113-31.

Country

USA.

Target group

Social work students.

Learning and teaching about assessment

Students conduct neighbourhood assessments in groups, having been given guidelines as to the types of information they should be collecting. This assignment is undertaken as part of a course on groupwork taken within the university.

Evaluation

Students were enthusiastic and gave overwhelmingly favourable course evaluations.

Reference

Robson, K. and Savage, A. (2001) 'Assessing adult attachment: interview course with Patricia Crittenden, November 2000-April 2001', *Child Abuse Review*, vol 10, pp 440-7.

Country

England.

Target group

Practitioners who work with victims and perpetrators of child abuse.

Learning and teaching about assessment

This was a three-module 18-day course facilitated by Dr Patricia Crittenden from Miami, USA between November 2000 and April 2001 about assessing adult attachment, with participants being trained in the use of the Adult Attachment Interview (AAI). Participants learnt how to conduct the interviews. Discourse analysis was taught and interviews were transcribed, analysed and coded. It was assumed that participants already had some basic awareness of attachment theory and back reading was provided prior to the course. Module 1 concentrated on learning to read and classify transcripts of non-clinical populations. Module 2 consisted of transcripts from people more likely to come to the attention of professionals. Module 3 built on the information from the previous modules, dealing with clinical transcripts including people who were diagnosed as having depressed, disorganised and reorganised modifiers. Days were structured into two segments. In the morning participants worked on reading and classifying transcripts which were then discussed with Dr Crittenden in the afternoon.

Evaluation

This paper is an evaluation of the course by two participants.

Reference

Rumsey, H. (2000) 'Learning risk assessment in South Africa: issues of language power and imperialism', *Social Work Education*, vol 19, pp 207-18.

Country

South Africa.

Target group

Child protection professionals from social work, health, police and education.

Learning and teaching about assessment

A programme of cooperation between the Institute of Child and Family Development based at the University of Western Cape and the School of Social Studies based at University College Chichester resulted in an English academic running a two-day course on risk assessment with child protection professionals in South Africa in November 1998. The course covered principles of practice; the importance of keeping an accurate account of events; the need to ensure ongoing contact and communications with parents and children; the need to ensure that frontline practitioners are experienced, have expertise in, and commitment to child protection work and are well supervised; the need for those carrying out the assessments to avoid sexist, culturalist and ageist assumptions; and the need to involve other professionals and to ensure good communication between them in the assessment process. An interactive teaching methodology was adopted in which teachers become both facilitators of other's learning and learners themselves.

Evaluation

This paper is predominantly the author's reflection on teaching in a foreign culture. Formal and informal feedback was sought at the end of the course, and at the time of writing there was ongoing research around the development of risk assessment in participants' workplaces.

Reference

Stanley, N. and Manthorpe, J. (1997) 'Risk assessment: developing training for professionals in mental health work', *Social Work and Social Sciences Review*, vol 7, pp 26-38.

Country

England.

Target group

Professionals in mental health work.

Learning and teaching about assessment

Two half-day sessions on risk management were delivered to a group of 20 mental health workers in the setting of a short course on the discharge of mentally disordered people and their continuing care in the community. Training was designed by social services training staff following consultation with local user groups, mental health practitioners and managers. Participants were taught how to use a structured tool to perform risk assessments.

Evaluation

Postal questionnaire on completion of course and longer-term benefits explored three months later.

Reference

Sullivan, R. and Clancy, T. (1990) 'An experimental evaluation of interdisciplinary training in intervention with sexually abused adolescents', *Health and Social Work*, vol 15, pp 207-14.

Country

USA.

Target group

Health professionals.

Learning and teaching about assessment

Californian legislation requires that those providing services to children and families must have training in the recognition and assessment of child abuse and in the reporting procedures used to initiate investigations and intervention on behalf of these children. The state contracted with an independent training organisation that designed and implemented a series of one-day training sessions throughout the state. Objectives of the training: improve health practitioners' ability to identify indicators of sexual abuse in the adolescents they serve; increase the number of interviewing techniques available to health practitioners in approaching this subject with adolescent patients; increase the likelihood of health practitioners making appropriate referrals to mandated child protection and law enforcement agencies. A lecture and discussion format adopted with some experiential exercises included to teach participants interviewing techniques.

Evaluation

Independent evaluation of the training was required as a condition of the contract. The evaluation consisted of pre- and post-test measures of knowledge about indicators of child abuse.

Reference

Tanner, K. (1999) 'Observation: a counter culture offensive. Observation's contribution to the development of reflective social work practice', *International Journal of Infant Observation*, vol 2, no 2, pp 12-32.

Country

England.

Target group

Social work students.

Learning and teaching about assessment

Reports on the learning opportunities gained by involvement in child observation as part of the DipSW programme at Goldsmiths College.

Evaluation

Extensive feedback from students as to how the process of observation stimulated learning is provided.

Reference

Tanner, K. and le Riche, P. (1995) '"You see but you do not observe": the art of observation and its application to practice teaching', *Issues in Social Work Education*, vol 15, no 2, pp 66-80.

Country

England.

Target group

Social work students.

Learning and teaching about assessment

Students at Goldsmiths College undertake 10 observations of a young child and participate in weekly seminars at which they present their observations, and discuss what issues emerge from their observation.

Evaluation

No evaluation.

Reference

Taverner, D. Dodding, C.J. and White, J.M. (2000) 'Comparison of methods for teaching clinical skills in assessing and managing drug-seeking patients', *Medical Education*, vol 34, pp 285-91.

Country

Australia.

Target group

Medical students.

Learning and teaching about assessment

As part of a programme of teaching assessment skills in relation to drug-dependent clients to medical students, students were allocated to either a didactic tutorial, a tutorial in which four doctor–patient interactions were included in a 20-minute video which were then discussed by the class, and a computer-aided instruction package which included sections of the video clips and multiple choice questions with branching according to answers given. All options took place within a 60-minute timetabled session.

Evaluation

No difference in the examination results was found between students who tested this material and between those who attended the different types of sessions. Students, however, expressed a preference for the video.

Reference

Thornton, S. and Garrett, K.J. (1995) 'Ethnography as a bridge to multicultural practice', *Journal of Social Work Education*, vol 31, pp 67-74.

Country

USA.

Target group

Social work students.

Learning and teaching about assessment

Through teaching students skills in ethnographic research, it is expected that they will become more sensitive observers of other cultures and be able to form assessments that are culturally relevant.

Evaluation

Evaluation of whole programme includes pre- and post-course self-assessment of culturally sensitive practice. Student evaluations of this aspect of the programmer were very positive.

___

Reference

Trautmann, F. and Burrows, D. (2000) 'Conditions for effective use of rapid assessment and response methods', *International Journal of Drug Policy*, vol 11, pp 59-61.

Country

Russia.

Target group

Health workers.

Learning and teaching about assessment

An 11-day course in rapid assessment techniques is followed by participants conducting a rapid assessment over 12 weeks, and concludes with a further five days of input on response development. Training courses include discussions of the concepts underpinning public health and HIV prevention, training in research methods and exercises to prepare participants to implement their findings. Facilitators visit participants during the 12-week project and assist in arranging other supports needed to undertake the project.

Evaluation

This paper is the authors' reflection on their experience of running these courses in Russia.

___

Reference

Van Voorhis, R.M. (1998) 'Culturally relevant practice: a framework for teaching the psychosocial dynamics of oppression', *Journal of Social Work Education*, vol 34, pp 121-33.

Country

USA.

Target group

Social work students.

Learning and teaching about assessment

A framework for assessing the effects of oppression on individuals, families and groups is proposed. In addition to using case studies, the author suggests that social work educators could encourage students to use the framework to explore the experiences of oppressed people recorded in literature including biographies and autobiographies as well as short stories and fiction.

Evaluation

No evaluation provided. It is proposed that the teaching can be evaluated by reviewing assessments students conduct while involved in supervised practice learning in agency settings. If this is not possible, it is suggested that students could assess and plan an intervention for someone in a book, film or play.

Reference

Walsh, T.C. (2002) 'Structured process recording: a comprehensive model that incorporates the strengths perspective', *Social Work Education*, vol 21, pp 23-34.

Country

USA.

Target group

Social work students.

Learning and teaching about assessment

Structured process recordings are proposed as a tool for promoting assessment skills.

Evaluation

None.

Reference

Watkins, R.L. (2001) 'Using geographic information system (GIS) technology to integrate research into the field practicum', *Journal of Technology in Human Services*, vol 18, pp 135-54.

Country

USA.

Target group

Social work students.

Learning and teaching about assessment

Small numbers of social work students were trained in using geographic information systems that they could use in research projects to map information about agencies they were placed in. In particular, it enabled students to map perceptions versus actual data, such as in relation to client demographics or actual incidence of a range of community problems. The system used enabled integration of US census data, agency records and other survey data.

Evaluation

Reflections on the process and some of the issues that emerged are presented from the perspective of one of the facilitators.

Reference

Weinstein, J. (1994) 'A dramatic view of groupwork', *Groupwork*, vol 7, pp 248-55.

Country

England.

Target group

Social work students.

Learning and teaching about assessment

Discusses the use of films for teaching about group functioning and group assessment. Examines four films and/or books: *One Flew Over the Cuckoo's Nest, She'll be Wearing Pink Pyjamas, Lord of the Flies*, and *Dead Poets Society*. The author notes that care needs to be taken in selecting examples, as three of these examples focus exclusively on the experiences of men or boys and all assume the norms and values of white society.

Evaluation

None.

Reference

Wilkinson, I. (2000) 'The Darlington Family Assessment System: clinical guidelines for practitioners', *Journal of Family Therapy*, vol 22, pp 211-24.

Country

England.

Target group

Health and welfare professionals.

Learning and teaching about assessment

Mixed professional groups took 18-hour courses in the use of Darlington Family Assessment System (DFAS). The author claims the DFAS can be used as a training device in child mental health work. Clinical guidelines cover four areas.

Evaluation

The evaluation is of DFAS as an assessment tool rather than evaluating learning and teaching about assessment.

Reference

Will, R. and Forsythe, J. (1993) 'Family theatre: an interdisciplinary strategy for teaching family assessment', *Nurse Education Today*, vol 13, pp 232-6.

Country

Canada.

Target group

Nurses completing a 2-year post-registration diploma programme.

Learning and teaching about assessment

A collaboration with the university's drama programme resulted in groups of drama students role playing families for the nursing students to interview, assess and plan for care.

Evaluation

Author's evaluation of the use of the simulations to meet the objectives of the programme.

Reference

Wissmann, J.L. (1996) 'Strategies for teaching critical thinking in pharmacology', *Nurse Educator*, vol 21, pp 42-6.

Country

USA.

Target group

Nursing students.

Learning and teaching about assessment

Six strategies that have been used to teach and assess critical thinking skills in a pharmacology course are outlined. These are pharmacology connection tools; pharmacokinetics and pharmacodynamics; critical distinction among similar drugs; intraoperative awareness exercise; emergency room/intensive care unit pharmacologic decision-making practice; and an outcome assessment paper.

Evaluation

An indication of student feedback for each strategy is provided.

Appendix 2: Detailed methodology

To identify literature about the teaching of assessment in social work and cognate disciplines, we began by searching on-line versions of *Social Services Abstracts*, *Caredata* and *CINAHL* from those published in 1990 to those entered on the databases at the time of search in December 2002. These databases were selected on the basis that literature we were seeking would be most likely to be identified by using these databases, based on our experiences from previous research we have conducted about aspects of social work education. Due to time restrictions and financial considerations, the searches were restricted to documents in the English language.

The search terms used for *Social Services Abstracts* were:

- assess* and learn*;
- assess* and teach*; and
- assess* and train*.

The search terms used for *CINAHL* were:

- assess$ and learn$;
- assess$ and teach$; and
- assess$ and train$.

Caredata was searched using the keyword 'Assessment'.

All articles that were considered relevant were then sought. We supplemented this with a manual search, covering the same timeframe, of recent monographs and social work journals, held by the University of Glasgow and in our private libraries, which we know contain published articles on social work education in recent years. The journals reviewed were:

Australian Social Work (1990-2002);
Advances in Social Work and Welfare Education (1991-2000);
British Journal of Social Work (1990-2002);
European Journal of Social Work (1998-2002);
Issues in Social Work Education (1990-1999);

Journal of Social Work (2001–2002);
Journal of Social Work Education (1999–2002);
Journal of Social Work Practice (1990–2002);
Practice (1990–2002);
Research on Social Work Practice (1991–2002); and
Social Work Education (1990–2002).

As lengthy time lags between preparation and publication can result in information about the newest innovations not being widely available (Haynes, 1993), the editors of two key social work journals in the UK were contacted and asked if they could contact the authors of any in press papers which might be relevant for this review.

Many innovations in teaching are presented at social work education conferences, but many conference presentations are not subsequently published in academic or professional journals. For example, more than half (55%) of papers submitted to the Society for Academic Emergency Medicine meeting in 1991 did not eventuate in peer-reviewed journals within the following five years. Only 20% of those who had not published their findings had submitted articles and had them rejected. Interestingly there was no association between efforts to publish and factors such as quality of study, originality, sample size, design or results (Weber et al, 1998). As the authors of this report and their colleagues had copies of the abstracts from a number of social work education conferences in both the UK and beyond in recent years, these were searched in an attempt to identify relevant papers and their authors. The conference abstracts reviewed were:

- UK Joint Social Work Education Conference, Derby, July 2002;
- UK Joint Social Work Education Conference, Derby, July 2001;
- Joint Conference of the International Federation of Social Workers and International Association of Schools of Social Work, Montpelier, France, July 2002.
- Joint Conference of the International Federation of Social Workers and International Association of Schools of Social Work, Montreal, Canada, July–August 2000.

Another potential source of information about what social work educators were thinking or doing in relation to teaching of assessment were listservers managed by SWAPltsn. Archives of key electronic discussion lists were searched to identify any authors or educators to contact for further information. The discussion lists reviewed were:

- *Social Work learning and teaching and support network*
  www.jiscmail.ac.uk/lists/social-work-ltsn.html
  (March 2001–December 2002)
- *UKSOCWORK*
  www.jiscmail.ac.uk/lists/uksocwork.html
  (January 2000–December 2002)
- *International or comparative social work*
  www.jiscmail.ac.uk/lists/intsocwork.html
  (February 2000–December 2002)

Information about the study was placed on the SWAPltsn website in December 2002, inviting interested persons to contact the first author. On 13 January 2003, similar information about the project was distributed by email to all members of the JUCSWEC listserver. The text of this email was as follows:

Research Review of Teaching and Learning of Assessment in Social Work Education

This project, which is being conducted for the Social Care Institute for Excellence (SCIE) and the Social Policy and Social Work Learning and Teaching Support Network (SWAPltsn), aims to identify good practice in teaching and learning of assessment skills. In addition to a review of published literature, it is recognised that many professional innovations never receive widespread attention due to the promotion of ideas being to limited audiences, such as colleagues or conference attendees. Even if innovations do make it into more widely distributed books or journals, it can be some years before this occurs. Consequently, the research team is particularly interested in hearing from anyone who has been involved with innovations in the teaching of assessment, whether this be concerned with individuals, families, groups, carers or communities. A series of case studies is planned to showcase innovative teaching, and it is hoped that the various countries within the United Kingdom will be represented in these. If possible, we would like some of these case studies to involve partnerships with clients or other stakeholders such as employers.

Further information about this project, which is to be completed by April 2003, can be obtained from Dr Beth Crisp on 0141 330 6425 or at b.crisp@socsci.gla.ac.uk. The project team would also be delighted to receive any written information, such as conference papers or programme documentation which teaching and learning of assessment in social work and social care education. This can be forwarded to:

Dr Beth Crisp
Department of Social Policy and Social Work
University of Glasgow
Lilybank House
Bute Gardens
Glasgow G12 8RT

Further requests for more specific information were posted to the SWAPltsn and UKSOCWORK listservers on 11 February 2003. In particular, information was sought on methods of teaching assessment for which we had to that date been unable to find published accounts from within the UK. The text of this email was as follows:

Hi

I'm currently conducting a research review on the topic of how social work students are taught to make assessments of individuals, families, groups, carers and communities. I'm interested in hearing from anyone who has any had any involvement in innovations around the teaching and learning of assessment, especially in DipSW courses. In particular, I'd be interested in hearing from anyone who has been involved in programs which have involved:
- teaching assessment in partnership with local agencies
- teaching assessment to groups of students from both social work and other disciplines together
- problem based learning
- teaching rapid assessment methods
- using literature (novels, short stories, biographies) as case studies
- using standardised clients
- using geographic information systems
- any other innovations which you think others may find a worthwhile approach to the teaching of assessment

I can be contacted at the University of Glasgow on 0141 330 6425 or at b.crisp@socsci.gla.ac.uk and look forward to hearing from members of the list.

Beth Crisp
Dr Beth Crisp
Senior Lecturer
Department of Social Policy
University of Glasgow
Lilybank House
Bute Gardens
Glasgow G12 8RT
Scotland
+44 141 330 6425 (telephone)
+44 141 330 3543 (fax)

In response to these various efforts to publicise the project, a number of people made contact with the first author, some of whom provided the authors with further contacts, new references and/or unpublished details about how they teach assessment. Staff at SWAPltsn and colleagues of the authors provided additional names of UK social work educators who it was thought may be able to contribute ideas about the teaching of assessment.

Any relevant additional material identified by citation tracking were also sought. The various search strategies yielded an initial 183 journal articles for consideration, although only 60 were subsequently found to be about the process of teaching of assessment in social work and cognate disciplines. The remaining papers tended to be either about assessment per se, in which implications for the teaching of assessment could be explicit or implicit, or were more general papers about social work education.

To facilitate analysis, all relevant articles were classified under criteria including:

* country (England, Northern Ireland, Scotland, Wales, Australia, Canada, Hong Kong, Ireland, Israel, Russia, South Africa, US);
* target group for teaching about assessment (students or qualified workers from social work, nursing, medicine and so on);

93

- learning and teaching about assessment (what was taught and how); and
- evaluation (was the teaching of assessment evaluated?).

A draft report was prepared one month prior to the due date for the completion of this report and feedback sought from a small number of stakeholders. This included a focus group held with four experienced agency-based social work practitioners who are also involved in social work education in the West of Scotland. There was also a focus group with two members of service user forums who have experience of contributing service user perspectives in education to social and health professionals.

Index

V

value judgements 11
value systems
  of assessor 10
  of user 11
Van Voorhis, R.M. 14, 84–5
videos 18, 21, 83
vignettes 13
visits
  home-visiting techniques 71
  time for assessment 11, 32

W

Walsh, T.C. 85
Watkins, R.L. 85–6
Weinstein, J. 86
White, J.M. 83
WHO: Rapid Assessment and
  Response Guide on Injecting
  Drug Use 62–3, 84
Wilkinson, I. 86
Will, R. 87
Wissmann, J.L. 87
workshops 20
written assessments 23, 75

Other Knowledge Reviews available from SCIE

KNOWLEDGE REVIEW 2
The adoption of looked after children: A scoping review of research
Alan Rushton
1 904812 01 5
November 2003

KNOWLEDGE REVIEW 3
Types and quality of knowledge in social care
Ray Pawson, Annette Boaz, Lesley Grayson, Andrew Long and Colin Barnes
1 904812 02 3
November 2003

KNOWLEDGE REVIEW 4
Innovative, tried and tested: A review of good practice in fostering
Clive Sellick and Darren Howell
1 904812 03 1
November 2003

KNOWLEDGE REVIEW 5
Fostering success: An exploration of the research literature in foster care
Kate Wilson, Ian Sinclair, Claire Taylor, Andrew Pithouse and Clive Sellick
1 904812 04 X
November 2003